Contents

Glossary   **167**

THE MUSLIM 100

MUHAMMAD MOJLUM KHAN

ADAPTED BY IMRAN MOGRA

YOUNG ADULT EDITION

VOL.3

The Lives, Thoughts and Achievements of The Most Influential Muslims In History

The Muslim 100 YA Edition:
The Lives, thoughts and achievements of the
most influential Muslims in History.
Volume 3

First published by Kube Publishing Ltd,
Markfield Conference Centre
Ratby Lane, Markfield,
Leicestershire LE67 9SY

United Kingdom
Tel: +44 (0) 1530 249230
Website: www.kubepublishing.com
Email: info@kubepublishing.com

British Library Cataloguing-in-Publication Data

ISBN 978-1-84774-266-7 Paperback

ISBN 978-1-84774-267-4 Ebook

Cover Design: Amaan Ansari
Typesetting: LiteBook Prepress Services

Calligraphy: M. Swallay Mungly

Introduction

It goes without saying that societies across the world are experiencing changes at a very fast pace. We are living at a time when the world is interconnected, and instant communication has become normal. People who were once at the far corners of the world have virtually been brought together and can communicate immediately, perhaps to know one another better. One of the questions that this book invites you to think about is the extent to which you are aware of and connected to the history of Islam and Muslims. Are you a stranger to these great people who have left everlasting legacies for humanity?

Many educators, both Muslims and others, have realised the need to highlight and celebrate the huge contributions that Muslims have made over the centuries in the development of different subjects which gave the world the knowledge and means to improve life and civilisation. It is important for you to recognise that much of this history was deliberately suppressed, degraded, and doubted. Have you wondered why? In fact, there was a time when such history was absent "even among some universities and school syllabuses in may countries" You might want to ponder as to why this significant aspect of Muslim heritage and history of humanity was 'hidden'.

One the reasons may well be that it served the purposes of the powerful who wanted to keep their imperialist strategies and colonisation mission alive. Part of this mission involved the creation of a Muslim mind which felt inferior about itself and devalued its own knowledge, people, heritage, and lifestyle. Looking forward, this trend needs to be reversed, and Muslims need to take their rightful place on the world stage. Muslims and Islam matter. Therefore, it is my sincere hope that educational institutions will include this book in their libraries or as part of the syllabuses to enlighten their learners and to keep Islam's legacy alive.

The contribution of Muslims, as you will read, is a vast field and much has been written about it. Some of it remains in the Arabic language in libraries and in personal collections to be discovered by others and presented to the world. A lot of it has been ruined and continues to be destroyed through neglect, natural loss, modernisation, and wars.

In this book, you will find the fantastic contributions of Muslim scholars to literature, calligraphy, political administration, history, sociology, theology, finance and economy, philosophy, science, architecture, *hadith*, *tafsir*, *aqidah*, music, education, morality, mathematics, astronomy, medicine, chemistry, travel, logic, faith and spirituality. You will marvel at the physical geography of forts, palaces, mosques, mausoleums and libraries. You will also reflect upon some pleasant as well as unpleasant events and behaviours of individuals. This past will offer insights into what happened in previous centuries. As a historian, you will interpret the past for the benefit of the present and future.

You will be surprised with the interesting information about Muslim centres of learning which flourished in Europe, North Africa, the Middle East and Asia. You will come across some of the amazing libraries in Cordoba, Spain, established by generous patrons, which contained hundreds of thousands of books accessible to all. You are about to open the pages of the profiles of kings, saints, nobles, tyrants and people with questionable actions, morals and beliefs.

It has been said that history is a mirror of the people, and it is through this mirror of history that people see themselves and the performance of past peoples. As you turn the pages in this collection, you will encounter the photographic memory that some people had. For example, the compilers of *Hadith* literature memorised thousands of sayings of the Prophet Muhammad (ﷺ) and saved them for future generations. Muslims are forever indebted to them for preserving the lifestyle of the Prophet (ﷺ) for everyone. These narratives inform you about Muslim heritage so that you become conscious of your connections with your predecessors and hopefully give you a sense of direction for your life ahead.

Whilst you curiously examine these biographies, take note of the social history of the time and think about the trade links, commerce, travels, the lifestyle and other social characteristics of these historical periods. There are fascinating gems of information both in terms of facts and figures. Try to learn and remember some of these and share them with others. But you must see beyond these facts and probe into the cause and effects of the rise and fall of nations and their rulers.

Spirituality is a theme that runs through most of the lives of these remarkable people. In whatever they pursued, they did not ignore this critical aspect of their life, their relationship with Allah and their pursuit of achieving higher ideals in life. They always kept, in their mind and heart, the Hereafter as their final destination and prepared for it diligently. But they were not only concerned about themselves. They wished others to be mindful of Allah, to become better people and live in kindness with a view to eternal happiness. How did they achieve this?

These brilliant narratives will illustrate to you the preservation, reformation, revival and propagation of Islam and the different methodologies adopted by scholars, saints, activists, politicians, philanthropists, Imams, shaykhs and soldiers for this. They preserved the light of Islam in a variety of ways. They aimed to beautify (*ihsan*) characters, ethics and manners. They also aimed to purify (*tazkiya*) the heart and soul. They taught (*ta'lim*) knowledge. They converted and disseminated (*da'wah*) the message of Islam.

One of the most fascinating observations to make is that there is a universal characteristic that flows through these people as they belonged to different cultures, races, ethnicities and languages, and that they were were rich and poor, male and female. Actually, some were crippled, like Tamerlane, who was one of the world's greatest conquerors, and others were orphaned very young. Yet they achieved great accomplishments. Mothers have been the bedrock for the likes of Imam al-Bukhari and many others, as you will read.

As you study these short biographies, you will notice their sincerity, determination and humility in search of learning. This enabled them to travel to distant lands and sit at the feet of experts with different faiths, cultures and worldviews. In doing so, they learnt other local languages, translated books and critically evaluated other people's knowledge and truth claims. They then made this knowledge widely accessible.

You will also be exposed to some Muslim, Greek and other philosophical thoughts which may appear unfamiliar to you. As you read, you will understand that some of these civilisations are different from the Islamic civilisation, spirituality and morality. However, some understanding of this is necessary, without making generalisations about Western thought and modernism, because these ideals and ideas continue to influence the political, social, ethical, aesthetic and economical thought of the current modern world. You will also encounter the different thoughts and schools that exists among Muslims.

You will recognise that unity and justice were cornerstones for many of those leaders who were more successful in providing stability and security. These then facilitated the establishment of educational centres, hospitals and general public order. Once these were functioning and secure, the wellbeing and prosperity of their peoples and societies followed. On the other hand, exploitation, oppression, greed, nepotism, corruption, deception and disunity brought downfall. In other words, be curious as you dive into the past and arrive at an appreciation about the how and why of events.

You are living at a time when Western civilization and the powers associated with them are at the top. Muslim nations are weaker and controlled but Muslims have spiritual strength. This book will make you realise that the story of Muslims was once different and the direction that the world is taking can be changed. You need to take up this challenge to your heart to lead the world. "There is plenty to inspire you and for you to aspire to."

As you have a dialogue with this historical period, I sincerely hope that what you learn from this collection creates a love for further knowledge. I hope you will appreciate these figures' amazing achievements and that their legacy motivates you to greatness and the service of humanity. Nobody ever imagined that Islam, which was on verge of extinction during the night of *hijra,* would spread to all corners of the world and become a religion with over a billion followers. You are about to discover how that happened.

The biographies have been presented in a chronological order. It will help you to place the geography, personalities and events in a systematic order of history. From the school and curriculum perspective to grasp history well, an understanding of its chronology is important. The chronology will support you to develop a better mental framework of the past so that you have a secure grasp of the timeline of Islam as it has unfolded over the centuries. You should also be able to extend and deepen your knowledge and understanding of local and world history. This will provide you with a well-informed context for learning history in general. Register in your mind the younger age at which some of them died but how massive their success and impact has been. Overall, you will identify significant events, make connections, compare and contrast and analyse trends over centuries.

Imran Mogra
July 2025

54

Nizam al-Mulk
(b.1020 - d.1092 CE) /
(b.411 - d.485 AH)

There is no shortage of influential statesmen, humanitarians and educationalists in Islamic history. These remarkable people played a key role in the promotion of religious, philosophical and scientific learning in the Muslim world. Without their valuable contributions, the Muslim world would certainly have been much poorer in comparison with other great world civilisations. It is largely due to the vision and dedication of these great statesmen and philanthropists that the Islamic civilisation attained such dazzling heights in educational, cultural and artistic activities.

One Muslim statesman and educationalist played a far greater role in the rise and development of a world-class educational system in the Muslim world than probably any other. His love of knowledge and his desire to eliminate illiteracy throughout his territory led to the rise of a new and vibrant culture of learning across the Muslim world. As the founder and patron of the famous Nizamiyah Colleges, Nizam al-Mulk is today considered to be one of Islamic history's most celebrated educators.

Hasan ibn Ali al-Tusi, better known as Nizam al-Mulk, was born in Radhkan, a village in Tus in the Persian province of Khurasan, close to present-day Mashhad in Iran. The son of a Ghaznavid income collector, Nizam al-Mulk was brought up in a family where religious practices were thoroughly observed. His family members also valued educational and artistic activities most highly. During his early years, he studied Arabic language, grammar and *fiqh* (Islamic jurisprudence) in his native Radhkan. After completing his elementary education, he travelled to Nishapur where he received advanced training in Arabic and Persian literature, mathematics and traditional Islamic sciences under the guidance of distinguished scholars such as Shaykh Hibatullah.

In Nishapur, his classmates included Umar Khayyam (see chapter 55), the famous poet, scientist and mathematician and Hasan-i-Sabbah (b.1050 -d.1124 CE), the notorious founder of the neo-Isma'ili Assassin sect. According to the Persian historian Al-Tabib, the three of them became good friends during their student days and on one occasion they made a sincere promise that whichever of them attained success first would help the others. Some historians like Sayyid Sulayman Nadwi have questioned the authenticity of this story, but they do not dispute the fact that Nizam al-Mulk, Umar Khayyam and Hasan-i-Sabbah had studied together in Nishapur.

By the time Nizam al-Mulk had completed his advanced education, the political landscape in the Muslim world had shifted radically. Named after their ancestral leader Seljuk, the Turkish Oghuz clans converted to Islam in the eleventh century. Based in a region close to the north of the Caspian and Aral Sea, the Seljuk mobilised their political power and military might against their main rivals, the Ghaznavid and the Buwayhid dynasties. As a result, they inflicted crushing defeats on them in 1040 and 1060 CE respectively. Seljuks now became one of the Muslim world's most powerful political dynasties of the time.

After bringing back the traditional Caliphate in Baghdad, the Seljuks successfully prevented the Fatimid attempts to gain full control of the Muslim world. The Abbasid Caliph, Malik al-Rahim, was grateful to the Seljuks for defending the Abbasid Caliphate from Fatimid invasion. To reward him, the ruling Abbasid Caliph Malik al-Rahim officially crowned the first Seljuk ruler, Tughrul Beg, as the 'King of the East and West'. As for Nizam al-Mulk, he was twenty-eight at the time and began his career as a civil servant in the provincial administration of Adud al-Dawlah, better known as Alp Arsalan (the valiant lion), who was a nephew of Tughrul Beg.

55

Umar Khayyam
(b.1048 - d.1131CE) /
(b.440 - d.526 AH)

The period from the eighth to the sixteenth century is generally considered to be the age of Islamic supremacy. During this period, Muslims governed a significant part of Asia, Africa and Europe. Under the support of famous Muslim rulers like Harun al-Rashid (see chapter 28), al-Ma'mun (see chapter 33), Mahmud of Ghazna (see chapter 49), Nizam al-Mulk (see chapter 54), Sulayman the Magnificent (see chapter 79) and Akbar the Great (see chapter 80), the Muslim world was ahead of the rest of the world in educational, artistic and cultural pursuits. Not surprisingly, some of the greatest scientists, philosophers, writers and poets of the time were Muslims who, in turn, brought in a period of intellectual creativity and social and cultural progress across the Islamic world. Their contribution to the progress of human thought and culture later inspired the Europeans to throw off the captivity of feudalism and backwardness which ruled supreme across Europe at the time and follow the greatness and brilliance of Islamic civilisation at its height.

The tenth and eleventh centuries were, arguably, the most intellectually and culturally progressive periods in the history of Islam. It was during this era that some of the Muslim world's most influential scientists, philosophers, theologians and educationalists, like Ibn al-Haytham (see chapter 48), al-Biruni (see chapter 50), Ibn Sina (see chapter 52), Nizam al-Mulk (see chapter 54), al-Ghazali (see chapter 56) and Hakim Sana'i (b. 1080-d. 1131), lived and flourished. Umar Khayyam, who was a legendary astronomer and mathematician and one of the most famous Muslim poets in the Western world, also lived during this unusually creative period in the intellectual history of Islam.

Umar ibn Ibrahim Khayyam, better known as Umar (or Omar) Khayyam, was born in the Persian city of Nishabur. His ancestors belonged to an Arab tribe who were excellent tent-makers. But, following the Muslim conquest of Persia, his family moved to Nishapur where they also became successful tent merchants; hence the sur-name *al-khayyam* (the tent sellers). Unfortunately, historians like Ibn Khallikan (b. 1211-d. 1282 CE), and al-Kutubi (b. 1287-d. 1363 CE) do not say much about him in their works; thus, very little is known about Umar Khayyam's childhood and early education.

Imam Bayhaqi (b. 995-d. 1077 CE), the author of *Ta'rikh-i-Bayhaqi* (literally Bayhaqi's history), on the other hand, knew him well and recorded some information about his life and work. As one of the foremost centres of Islamic learning and trade, Nishapur attracted some of the leading scholars and theologians of the time who lived and taught there. Students thus flocked there from across Khurasan and the neighbouring regions to study under the guidance of these outstanding scholars. Umar Khayyam was brought up in a lower-middle-class family. He received his early education in Arabic, Persian and Qur'anic sciences under the guidance of his local teachers, such as *Qadi* al-Anbari. As a gifted student, he excelled in his studies and his teachers encouraged him to enrol at the renowned Nishapur College, where he mastered Arabic and Persian before developing a keen interest in mathematics, astronomy and the other physical sciences of his day. Impressed by his son's intellectual abilities, his father encouraged him to pursue higher education in mathematics and science.

As a leading educational institution, Nishapur College only attracted the brightest students. Thus, according to historians like Bayhaqi, some of Umar Khayyam's classmates at Nishapur College included Nizam al-Mulk (see chapter 54), who later became a celebrated educationalist and statesman within the Seljuk administration, and Hasan-i-Sabbah (b. 1050-d. 1124 CE), the future founder of the notorious extremist Isma'ili Assassin sect. Although some historians have questioned the authenticity of this story, they agree that the three of them had studied together. In fact, at Nishapur College they became good friends and on one occasion reportedly promised to help each other should any one of them attain a position of power. Like his friends, Umar Khayyam was a bright student but, unlike them, he was reserved and studious, and remained occupied with his studies. By contrast, Nizam al-Mulk was a natural-born politician. He soon rose to prominence within the Seljuk administration and appointed his former classmate, Hasan-i-Sabbah, to a high-ranking government post. But, being a cunning individual, Hasan fell out with Nizam al-Mulk and moved out of Seljuk areas. He then established the Assassin sect. From his base in the fortress of Alamut (situated towards the northeast of Qazwin), he and his followers masterminded assassination attempts on their enemies. Nizam al-Mulk and his Seljuk supporters were thus placed on the top of their target list.

Unlike Nizam al-Mulk and Hasan-i-Sabbah, who were very ambitious individuals, Umar Khayyam deliberately remained detached from politics and public life. Instead, he travelled in search of knowledge and visited some of the most famous centres of learning in Samarqand, Bukhara, Isfahan and Balkh. In so doing, he completed his advanced training in philosophy and science under the guidance of some of the leading scholars of his time. He then returned to Nishapur, where he began to teach mathematics and the physical sciences at his old college. In addition to mastering mathematics and science, Umar Khayyam attained considerable expertise in traditional Islamic sciences and was able to recite the Qur'an according to the seven traditional modes of *ahruf* (recitation).

He may not have been a direct student of Ibn Sina, but Umar Khayyam was thoroughly familiar with Ibn Sina's scientific and philosophical works. According to the historian Bayhaqi, Umar Khayyam was an Islamic philosopher in the tradition of Ibn Sina; he also found time to translate one of his works from Arabic to Persian. However, unlike Ibn Sina, Umar Khayyam did not write much, although he was an able and skilful teacher who later became very popular in and around Nishapur for his vast knowledge of science and philosophy. When his name and fame spread across Nishapur and Khurasan, Nizam al-Mulk, his old classmate at Nishapur College and now the Seljuk Prime Minister, invited him to Isfahan and offered him the influential post of chief scientific advisor to the government.

As an accomplished scientist who was renowned for his knowledge in astronomy, he was promoted to one of the highest posts within the Seljuk civil service. He worked closely with Nizam al-Mulk and advised the Seljuk ruler, Sultan Malik Shah (b.1055 -d. 1092 CE), on all the astronomical and scientific issues of the day. As wise rulers and great statesmen, both Malik Shah and Nizam al-Mulk were known for their love of learning and education. Thus, it was that they founded an astronomical observatory in Nishapur to promote and facilitate advanced scientific training and research. Umar Khayyam was appointed director of this observatory, where all the leading Muslim scientists and mathematicians of the day pursued their scientific training and research under his supervision.

As a gifted scientist and mathematician, Umar Khayyam thrived under Seljuk support as did his many colleagues. One of the fruits of their research was the *jalali* calendar. Named after their Seljuk ruler, Sultan Malik Shah, this calendar was more accurate than the Gregorian calendar produced in Rome in 1582 CE by Pope Gregory XIII. Not surprisingly, this calendar has remained the official calendar of Iran to this day. His other important contributions were in the field of mathematics where he conducted extensive research in different branches of mathematics and became one of the most original writers on algebra since al-Khwarizmi, the pioneer of Arabic algebra. Although Umar Khayyam wrote many books and essays on scientific, mathematical and philosophical topics, his most valuable work was the 'Treatise on Establishing the Problems of Integration and Equation'.

As the title suggests, the subject of this book was similar to that of al-Khwarizmi's original work on algebra, but the scope of this book was far greater. Umar divided it into ten different chapters with a fresh and comprehensive explanation of algebra and related topics. And in so doing he demonstrated that there was an underlying metaphysical link between mathematics and geometry, as indicated by ancient Greek writers like Euclid. As a master of Euclidean geometry, Umar critically reviewed this branch of early mathematics and published his research findings in a separate book entitled,

'Exposition of the Difficulties of Euclid's Elements'. Nevertheless, his 'Treatise on Establishing the Problems of Integration and Equation' is today considered to be one of the most important mathematical treatises of the early medieval period. After completing this book, he presented a copy to Nizam al-Mulk, who publicly praised him for his efforts and encouraged him to produce more works like it. Copies of this and other important mathematical and philosophical books authored by Umar Khayyam have been preserved in manuscript form at libraries in London, Paris and Leiden.

Umar was known in the East as a great astronomer and mathematician. However, he became most famous in the West as a poet mainly because of his *Ruba'iyyat* (collection of quatrains). It was first translated into English by the Victorian poet Edward Fitzgerald (b. 1809-d. 1883) in 1859 CE. The *Ruba'iyyat* of Omar Khayyam became an instant hit in the English-speaking world soon after its publication. According to Andrew Lang, who was a member of the 'Omar Khayyam Club of London' and a distinguished historian of English literature, the slim pamphlet of the 'Rubaiyat' was a 'drug in the market'. Then a wider circle of young university men made it an idol; to adore it was a sign of grace. In the long run, to admire Umar, it was no longer necessary to have read anything else.

Fitzgerald, who was born near Woodbridge in Suffolk, was an avid reader and a respected literary critic who produced some translations. It was his free interpretation of Umar Khayyam's Persian quatrains which earned him widespread literary praise. In the process, Umar Khayyam also became the most popular and admired Muslim poet in the West. Admittedly, Fitzgerald's translation is very beautiful and eloquent, but not free from error. Indeed, his portrayal of Umar Khayyam as a pleasure-seeking and self-indulgent poet who preferred women and wine over all other things in life was nothing short of an ugly misrepresentation of the man, who was not only a practising Muslim but also a Sufi sympathiser.

Having said that, although he had received training in traditional Islamic sciences, Umar Khayyam was not the average religious scholar. He explored the meaning and purpose of Islamic rituals to understand their 'inner' or 'spiritual' meanings. That is why, using colourful poetic language, he poked fun at people who wore the cloak of religiosity outwardly but failed to live by the moral, ethical and spiritual demands of their faith. Umar Khayyam's social criticism, moral dislike and philosophical doubt were therefore directed more towards the preachers – who preached but did not practisce themselves – rather than towards the faith itself. Indeed, far from being a champion of wild materialism, moral relativism and cultural pleasure-seeking, he was immersed in Islamic morality and *tasawwuf* (Islamic spirituality).

There are heated debates about the Islamic and heretical nature of some of his poems, but by all accounts, Umar Khayyam was an outstanding mathematician, astronomer, philosopher and poet. Not surprisingly, his groundbreaking contributions in these fields have influenced generations of famous Muslim, and non-Muslim, scholars, thinkers and poets including al-Ghazali, al-Tusi (see chapter 68), al-Samarqandi (b. 1250-d. 1310 CE), Mark Twain (b. 1835-d. 1910 CE), T.S. Eliot (b. 1888-d. 1965 CE), and Matthew Arnold (b. 1822-d. 1888 CE), among others.

After the brutal murder of his friend and patron, Nizam al-Mulk, by the followers of the Assassin sect of Hasan-i-Sabbah, he went to Makkah to perform the sacred *hajj* and on his return, he served the new Sultan Ahmad Sanjar for a period. He eventually resigned from his job as a scientific advisor to the Seljuk ruler of the time. He then took up his old teaching post at Nishapur College where he spent the rest of his life. Umar Khayyam died at the age of around eighty-three and was buried in his native Nishapur.

56

Abu Hamid al-Ghazali (b.1058 - d.1111 CE) / (b.450 - d.505 AH)

The main sources of early Islamic thought and practice were the Qur'an and Prophetic *Sunnah*. But following the rapid expansion of Islam into Egypt, Persia and Syria, the Muslims – for the first time – came directly in contact with foreign ideas such as ancient Greek philosophy. This had a huge influence on Muslim scholars. As a result, Islamic thought began to represent itself in several different ways.

For a start, although Mu'tazilism initially emerged as a political movement, it later became an entirely rationalistic movement under the influence of Wasil ibn Ata as explained in the account of Hasan al-Basri (see chapter 15). Then there were the *falasifah* (the Muslim philosophers) who were influenced by Hellenistic thought. They created a largely philosophical interpretation of Islam. Moreover, under Imam Abul Hasan al-Ash'ari's guidance, *ilm al-kalam* (speculative theology) also became a powerful force within the Islamic intellectual community. Before that, under Hasan al-Basri's guidance, Sufism (Islamic spirituality) had become a powerful force in the Muslim world. These rationalistic, philosophical, theological and mystical trends continued to compete for the hearts and minds of Muslims until the unbeatable personality of Imam al-Ghazali appeared in the eleventh century. He championed and reasserted traditional Islamic thought and practices as never before.

Abu Hamid Muhammad ibn Muhammad al-Ghazali, known in the West as Algazel, was born in Tus in Khurasan (in present-day Mashhad in Iran). The city of Tus was the hub of Islamic learning and scholarship at the time. It was also the birthplace of the celebrated Sufi master al-Hujwiri, the outstanding poet Firdawsi (see chapter 47) and the renowned statesman Nizam al-Mulk (see chapter 54). Al-Ghazali's father was a devout Muslim, who died when his son was an infant. He and his brother Ahmad al-Ghazali were, therefore, raised by their mother. She ensured that her two sons received a good education. Al-Ghazali attended the class of a local Sufi tutor and attained expertise in Arabic language, grammar, Qur'an, *Hadith*, *fiqh* (jurisprudence), Sufi thought and poetry before he was fifteen.

He then conducted a detailed study of *fiqh* under the guidance of leading experts on the subject, at the seminary in Jurjan. He was seventeen when he completed his study of *fiqh* and returned home to Tus to continue his higher education. Al-Ghazali was a gifted student who needed minimal guidance from his tutors. His unusual ability to understand complex ideas and thoughts enabled him to absorb the principles and practices of Islam easily.

He was only about twenty years old when he travelled to Nishapur to pursue advanced education in Islamic sciences. He was fortunate to study *ilm al-kalam* (Islamic theology) and *fiqh* under *imam al-haramayn* al-Juwayni. Imam al-Juwayni was an outstanding follower of Ash'arite theology. He was also one of the foremost Islamic scholars of his generation and lectured at the famous Nizamiyah College in Nishapur. Al-Ghazali sat at the feet of this master and became one of his favourite students. Like al-Juwayni, he became an Ash'arite theologian and a Shafi'i *faqih* (jurist).

It was al-Juwayni who introduced him to *mantiq* (the science of logic) and the philosophical thought of the *falasifah* (Muslim philosophers). However, it was al-Ghazali's intellectual brilliance and analytical ability which impressed al-Juwayni the most; so much so that he nominated him to become his teaching assistant. This established al-Ghazali's credentials and increased his new reputation as a young Islamic scholar. It was during this period that he composed his famous book 'The Sifted Notes on the Methods of

Fundamentals'. In it, he elaborated on the fundamental principles of Islamic law and legal methodology.

As a leading centre of Islamic learning, Nishapur also attracted eminent Sufi personalities who lived there. They taught the knowledge of Islamic spirituality and *batini* (inner) sciences to their followers. Al-Ghazali also attended *zawiyah* (Sufi lodges). He received training in the theoretical and practical dimensions of Sufism under the guidance of al-Farmadhi, who was a respected Sufi personality of Nishapur and a pupil of the famous Imam al-Qushayri. In 1085 CE al-Juwayni died and al-Ghazali was asked to become a professor of Islamic thought at the Nizamiyah College in Baghdad by the Nizam al-Mulk himself. Nizam was the great Prime Minister of the Seljuk Empire and founder of the Nizamiyah College.

At the age of around thirty-four, he became the youngest professor at Nizamiyah. This was an extraordinary honour for young al-Ghazali since the Nizamiyah College of Baghdad was the Oxford or Harvard of its time. As soon as al-Ghazali started teaching *fiqh*, *kalam* and *Hadith* at Nizamiyah, his name and fame began to spread across the Islamic dominion and Nizam al-Mulk became his patron. Nizam regularly consulted him on all the important religious and political issues. Al-Ghazali's daily lectures at Nizamiyah became so popular that up to three hundred students came to listen to him at a time. However, just when he thought he had achieved all that was possible for someone so young to achieve, he suddenly found himself stranded in the middle of an intellectual crisis.

This crisis made al-Ghazali restless. Being naturally inquisitive, and sceptical of received wisdom, he thrived in the lion's den. He questioned everything and, in the process, left no stone unturned. He was deeply disturbed by the apparent conflict between the views of the rationalists and the traditionalists. The rationalists argued that *aql* (human reason) was superior to *wahy* (revelation). The traditionalists considered Divine revelation to be infallible and, therefore, it was more authoritative compared to the fallible human reason. Al-Ghazali was not a philosopher, but he had studied philosophical thought during his time with his teacher al-Juwayni. This enabled him to understand and evaluate the various strands of philosophical and theological thought which existed in the Muslim world at the time. His observations disturbed him intensely and made him very restless. He discovered that a huge range of religious sects and groups had emerged that promoted their own sets of doctrines and beliefs. He felt these were heretical and directly contradicted traditional Islamic teachings and practices. So, how was he to determine which group was right and which one was wrong in the face of these diverse claims and counterclaims?

This prompted al-Ghazali to resign from Nizamiyah College and study all the well-known religious sects and groups. During his studies, he became aware of the limitations of existentialism and rationalism. Existentialism is a belief that states that people are responsible for creating their own purpose and meaning in life and that individuals have the freedom to make their own choices. He found both to be unreliable categories for reaching the Truth. The more al-Ghazali questioned, the more he doubted the foundation of knowledge. Thus, for a period, he became a complete sceptic, living in a state of doubt and depression. However, it should be noted here that his doubt was not the opposite of faith. In fact, it was an integral part of faith because his scepticism did not lead him to doubt the existence of Allah. Yet, it is true that he found himself stranded in an intellectual no-man's land. He found no comfort in rational arguments or logical proofs as a means of solving his predicament.

That was when he claimed to have been saved by the ray of *nur* (Divine light) which entered his heart and delivered him from his intellectual dilemma. Al-Ghazali considered this to be a gift from Allah Who had chosen to guide him to the *sirat al-mustaqim* (straight path). This brought much-needed peace and solace to his tortured mind and body as he affirmed the superiority of prophetic revelation and intellectual insight over human rationality. At peace with himself and reassured of the authenticity of his approach to Islam, he now continued his study of all the religious sects and groups to discover the truth for himself.

He began by studying and analysing the works of the *mutakallimun* (scholastic theologians), the *falasifah* (philosophers), the *ta'limiya* (Ta'limites or doctrinaires), and the Sufis (Islamic spiritual mentors or *mutasawwifin*). He studied scholastic theology at Nizamiyah College, so he was also familiar with this subject. Nevertheless, he undertook a fresh analysis of its basic principles and discovered that it had major shortcomings. Al-Ghazali found no common ground on which all theologians could agree. He argued, therefore, that scholastic theology would be of no value to anyone unless they believed in the vitalness of human reason. During this period, he authored many books on theology, before researching philosophy.

For the next three years, he conducted a thorough study of *falsafah* (Islamic philosophy). Through extensive research, he became fully knowledgeable about the works of the philosophers including those of great Muslim philosophers like al-Farabi (see chapter 41) and Ibn Sina (see chapter 52). He considered their ideas to be confused and misguided. The outcome of his study of philosophy was a book, 'The Intentions of the Philosophers', which al-Ghazali served as an introduction to his famous book, 'The Refutation of the Philosophers'.

In this book, he systematically analysed and rejected the *mashsha'iyah* (Peripatetic philosophy) as proposed by al-Farabi and Ibn Sina. In his book, he explained that he intended to free Islamic thought from the grip of Greek philosophy. By refuting the errors and heresies of the philosophers, he hoped to safeguard the public from doubt and confusion. Al-Ghazali's attack on Peripatetic philosophy proved so successful that Greek philosophical thought never managed to re-emerge in the Muslim world in a significant way after that. He single-handedly accomplished a task which even a group of gifted intellectuals would have struggled to achieve. By all accounts, this was a truly remarkable achievement. Astonishingly, al-Ghazali was only thirty-six when he authored his hugely influential book.

After philosophy, al-Ghazali turned his attention to a doctrinaire sect called the Ta'limites. This group believed that an 'infallible teacher' would one day appear and restore peace and order throughout the land. Al-Ghazali studied the beliefs and doctrines of this sect and refuted their claims in his books, 'The Infamies of the Batinites and the Virtue of the Mustazhirites'. It sparked a huge debate between al-Ghazali and the supporters of this sect. After this, he immersed himself in the ocean of Sufi thought and practices. Following a thorough study of the works of prominent Sufis like al-Muhasibi, Junaid al-Baghdadi, al-Shibli and al-Bistami, al-Ghazali realised that 'empirical' – as opposed to 'theoretical' – knowledge was the foundation of Sufism. This prompted him to abandon all worldly pleasures and dive himself wholeheartedly into the vast ocean of Sufism. But then he experienced another crisis. This time he suffered a serious nervous breakdown which badly affected his physical health, and he also developed speech problems.

According to al-Ghazali, his situation did not improve until Allah again delivered him from his problem by illuminating his heart with the spirit of truth. Now he was able to differentiate between 'theoretical' knowledge and 'experiential' knowledge. From now on, he devoted all his time and energy to seeking experiential knowledge to move closer to Divine nearness like the Sufis. He felt that endless theological debates, philosophical hair-splitting and heretical interpretations of Islamic beliefs and principles were unlikely to bring about peace and happiness in this life, or success in the hereafter. He found peace of mind and intellectual reassurance in the message of Sufism.

Imam al-Ghazali left Baghdad in 1095 CE at the age of thirty-seven to perform hajj. He returned to his native Tus around 1100 CE. On arrival, he was recalled to Nishapur by Fakhr al-Mulk to teach at the Nizamiyah College. He wrote many influential books during this period, including his famous autobiography, 'Deliverance from Error', and completed his voluminous *Ihya Ulum al-Din* (The Revivification of the Religious Sciences). In the latter, he presented a detailed and stimulating ethical overview of Islamic teachings covering all aspects of life. This book established al-Ghazali's reputation as one of the Muslim world's most gifted scholars and thinkers.

Moreover, his religious thoughts have influenced some of the most renowned Muslim scholars, intellectuals, Sufis and religious reformers. His philosophical and theological views also exerted considerable influence on renowned Jewish and Christian thinkers like St. Thomas Aquinas, Ramon Llull, Blaise Pascal and Musa bin Maimon, better known as Moses Maimonides. Al-Ghazali eventually returned to his native Tus and died at the age of fifty-three. He was buried in the cemetery close to the village of Sanabad, today located in the province of Isfahan, Iran.

57

Abd al-Qadir al-Jilani (b.1077 - d.1166 CE) / (b.470 - d.562 AH)

It would not be an exaggeration to say that the Muslim world has produced some of the world's great spiritual teachers who devoted their entire lives to acquiring a better understanding of the meaning and purpose of creation, and humankind's role in this vast universe. Unlike the philosophers, theologians and scientists, their method was to 'experience' knowledge. According to them, the universe and the human soul are not mere mental and abstract concepts which are independent of each other. They maintained that at a certain level, all things are interconnected and interdependent. They are all ultimately connected to a common denominator.

These great spiritual teachers were eager to understand the true nature of reality. They tried to go beyond the 'exterior' words and dived into the ocean of 'inner' meanings of things to attain 'experiential' knowledge. They believed that the 'experiential' knowledge would enable them to move closer to Allah – the origin of all that exists. One of the Muslim world's most influential, and arguably the most revered, Sufi (spiritual teacher and guide) was Shaykh Abd al-Qadir al-Jilani.

Shaykh Abd al-Qadir al-Jilani was born in the village of Nif, near Jilan in the province of Tabaristan, located on the coast of the

Caspian Sea. His family traced their lineage back to Hasan, the eldest son of Caliph Ali and a grandson of the Prophet. Abu Salih, his father, was a spiritual person and died when he was a child, but his remarkably religious mother, Umm al-Khair Fatimah, raised Abdul Qadir with the support of her scholarly and saintly father, Abdullah al-Suma'i, who claimed to be a descendant of Husayn, the son of Caliph Ali. Abd al-Qadir received his early education in Arabic, committed the whole Qur'an to memory and studied *Hadith* at home under the supervision of his mother and maternal grandfather. He then began his formal education at a local school when he was about ten. Thereafter, he pursued his intermediate studies at his local religious seminaries and acquired a sound knowledge of traditional Islamic sciences and Sufism (Islamic spirituality) before he reached his eighteenth birthday.

Abd al-Qadir left his native Jilan and journeyed to Baghdad, which was the capital of the Muslim world at the time. However, on his way to Baghdad, his caravan was surrounded by a group of robbers who confiscated the travellers' belongings by force. When one of the robbers asked young Abd al-Qadir if he had any valuables on him, to the surprise of the robber, he said his mother had stitched forty gold coins up his sleeves. At first, the robber did not take him seriously, probably because he thought the youngster was pulling his leg. But when the leader of the gang questioned Abd al-Qadir and demanded to see the hidden gold coins, he opened his sleeves and showed him the money. The robbers found his actions both puzzling and very unusual, to say the least. When they asked him why he admitted to having the gold coins, to their amazement, he replied that his mother's last words to him were that he must always speak the truth. Since denying that he had any money on him would have been to utter a falsehood, he decided to tell the truth, he said. Abd al-Qadir's truthfulness and honesty stirred the robbers' consciences and they fell to the ground and begged for his forgiveness and mercy. After thanking him for teaching them a lesson in good behaviour, ethics and morality, the robbers returned all the goods they had seized from the people and promised to change their ways.

After a long and eventful journey, he finally reached Baghdad. At the time Baghdad was a flourishing centre of Islamic learning and commercial activity. He also found the people of Baghdad very friendly and hospitable. Although joining the Baghdad branch of the famous Nizamiyah College (see chapter 54) would have been a better option, he decided not to join this college. Instead, he studied Arabic grammar, literature, *tafsir* (Qur'anic commentary), *Hadith* and *fiqh* (Islamic jurisprudence), especially *Hanbali fiqh*, under the guidance of Baghdad's leading scholars and teachers. He paid for his educational and maintenance costs out of the forty gold coins his mother had given him. But when the money ran out, he began to experience considerable financial and personal hardship. His financial situation became so desperate that he was not always able to afford to eat.

Despite these hardships, he remained determined to complete his advanced education. Known for his love of Prophetic traditions, Abd al-Qadir began to study *Hadith* literature under the supervision of expert *muhaddithun* (traditionists). During this period, he also studied Arabic literature under the guidance of al-Tabrizi, who was an expert on Arabic literature and the principal of Baghdad's famous Nizamiyah College. In addition, Abd al-Qadir received thorough training in *Hanbali* legal thought under the instruction of Baghdad's leading *Hanbali fuqaha* (jurists), Abu Sa'id Mubarak.

After completing his formal education, he sat at the feet of Shaykh Hammad al-Dabbas who was illiterate, but a prominent expert on Islamic spirituality Abd al-Qadir received training in Sufism from him. Under Shaykh al-Dabbas's instruction, he learned the theories and methods of Sufism and also became exposed to a new universe of meaning, purpose and spiritual fulfilment. This is when the 'inner' meaning and implication of religious teachings became clear to him for the first time. The move from the 'text' to the 'spirit of the text' enabled him to purify his soul and continue his quest for spiritual development and fulfilment.

Being a Sufi himself, the *Hanbali* jurist Abu Sa'id also played a decisive role in Abd al-Qadir's early journey for spirituality and fulfilment. He guided him in the methods and practices of Sufism, until the Abd al-Qadir had attained complete mastery of Islamic spirituality. After that, Abu Sa'id awarded him the robe to initiate others into Sufism. During this period Abd al-Qadir earned his livelihood by cultivating crops and vegetables, and he only spoke when it was required. After living within the ruins of Mada'in (Ctesiphon) like a hermit for eleven years, at the age of forty, he finally returned to Baghdad where he soon established his reputation as a gifted scholar of the Qur'an, Prophetic traditions, *Hanbali* jurisprudence and practitioner of Sufism. This prompted the locals to appoint him head of the same madrasah (Islamic seminary) where his former mentor Abu Sa'id once served as principal.

According to Abd al-Qadir, it was during this period that the Prophet Muhammad visited him in a dream and advised him to preach Islam and correct the locals. At the time he was busy lecturing on the religious sciences at the local seminary, without showing any desire or inclination to become a social activist and popular propagator of Islam. However, his encounter with the Prophet and the encouragement he received from Khwajah Yusuf Hamdani, a notable holy person of Baghdad, prompted him to begin delivering public lectures on all aspects of Islamic thought and practice. The aim was to encourage and inspire the locals to lead a more Islamic life based on the teachings of the Qur'an and *Sunnah*.

As a prominent scholar of traditional Islamic sciences and master of Islamic spirituality, Shaykh Abd al-Qadir was able to interpret Islamic teachings in a traditional, yet spiritually enhancing way so that both the traditionalist scholars and the Sufis used to sit side by side to listen to his inspiring lectures on all aspects of Islam, without raising any objections. His remarkable and unique ability to combine Islamic traditionalism with Islamic spirituality made him a hugely popular figure during his lifetime. If Imam al-Ghazali (see chapter 56) played an important role in intellectually harmonising traditional Islam with Sufism, then the credit for fully explaining this combination – to the religious scholars, Sufis and the public – goes to Abd al-Qadir.

According to his biographers, he became such a popular lecturer that the college grounds where he used to deliver his talks regularly overflowed, as thousands of people flocked from in and around Baghdad to hear him speak. Thanks to his intellectual brilliance and unique style of delivery, hundreds of non-Muslims (including Jews and Christians) embraced Islam and thousands of ordinary Muslims began to take their faith seriously. To accommodate the large crowds attending his lectures, the houses adjacent to his college were later purchased and demolished to create more space for the people.

Indeed, he became one of the first Sufi scholars in the history of Islam to acquire such a mass following. His ability to surpass theological differences and sectarian barriers encouraged the leading religious scholars, jurists, mystics, preachers and even the politicians of his day to set their differences aside and unite under the banner of Islam. He used to deliver lectures three times a week: on Friday morning before the weekly *salat al-jumu'ah*; on Tuesday evening, and also on Sunday mornings. More than seventy thousand people used to attend his lectures at any one time and around four hundred scribes used to write down his talks for the benefit of future generations.

Shaykh Abd al-Qadir enjoyed such success and popularity because he was able to combine practical Islam with its spiritual dimension. Not surprisingly, he did not consider himself to be either concerned only with inner matter or outer actions only. He did not believe in one without the other. To him both were necessary. Though he was a strict follower of the Prophetic practices, he also found time to engage in spiritual retreats. He emphasised the importance of leading a balanced and moderate lifestyle, focusing on the need to purify one's heart, mind and thought. Like Ma'ruf al-Karkhi and al-Junayd al-Baghdadi, Abd al-Qadir was a 'serious' Sufi, who strictly avoided the path of 'intoxication' taken by other Sufis like al-Bistami and al-Hallaj (see chapter 40). By doing this he restored the authentic practices of the Prophet.

As it happens, Abd al-Qadir was one of the most meticulous followers of the Prophetic *Sunnah*. Unlike many other Sufis, he married, even if it was late in life – at the age of fifty-one – and he ensured his personal and family life were regulated strictly following the teachings of the Prophet. Indeed, he refused to eat a meal if it was not prepared by following the Prophetic *Sunnah*. His contribution to the revival of Prophetic *Sunnah*, as well as Islamic spirituality, thus earned him the much-desired title of *muhyi al-din* (the 'reviver of Islam') during his lifetime.

Thanks to his group of dedicated scribes, Abd al-Qadir's lectures were preserved in the form of books and manuscripts for the benefit of future generations. They include 'That Which is Sufficient to the Seekers of True Path' and 'Disclosure of the Unseen'.

In total, more than twenty-four books have been attributed to Abd al-Qadir. According to his biographers, some of these books are not his works; they have been wrongly attributed to him by other people. Inspired by the Qur'an and Prophetic wisdom, Abd al-Qadir argued that humans were a creation of Allah, Who created them only to serve Him. Abd al-Qadir did not consider Allah to be a theological construct or a logical abstract; rather, he believed, Allah is One, Who resides in our hearts and continues to influence us in every sphere of our life – both individually as well as collectively – so that humans can experience Divine grace, mercy and compassion in this life and the hereafter, guided as ever by the supreme example and personality of the Prophet.

Shaykh Abd al-Qadir's unique and hugely influential interpretation of Islamic spirituality led to the emergence of one of the most powerful spiritual movements in the history of Islam. Named after him, the *qadiriyah* Sufi Order is today followed by millions of people throughout the Muslim world. The majority of the Sufi theoreticians and practitioners who came after him were one way or another influenced by his religious ideas and spiritual practices. These include Khwajah Mu'in al-Din Chishti (see chapter 62), Shihab al-Din Abu Hafs Umar al-Suhrawardi and Muhyi al-Din ibn al-Arabi (see chapter 65). He was aware of his immense influence and standing so Shaykh Abd al-Qadir himself once remarked, 'My foot is on the head of every saint.' He died at the venerable age of around eighty-nine and was buried in Abbasid Baghdad.

58

Ibn Tufayl
(b.1101 - d.1185 CE) /
(b.495 - d.581 AH)

Ancient Greek, Persian and Indian science and philosophy first entered the Muslim world during the eighth century and found their finest expression in the works of al-Kindi (see chapter 35) and Abu Bakr al-Razi (see chapter 39) in the ninth century and in that of al-Farabi (see chapter 41) and *ikhwan al-safa* (The Brethren of Purity) in the tenth. This then peaked in the works of the great Neoplatonist Ibn Sina in the eleventh century. As the philosophical sciences gained popularity across the Muslim world and began to challenge the traditional Islamic worldview, the amazing figure of Imam al-Ghazali (see chapter 56) emerged during the latter part of the eleventh century to launch a severe attack on the Neoplatonic school of Ibn Sina and al-Farabi. Al-Ghazali's intellectual assault on the Neoplatonic ideas as developed in his famous book, 'The Refutation of the Philosophers', struck a major blow against philosophical thought in general, and Neoplatonism in particular.

As expected, his successful rejection of philosophy delighted the Ash'arites and the Hanbalites who strongly opposed Neoplatonic thought. However, it seriously undermined the progress of philosophical thinking in the Islamic world. When philosophy was in full withdrawal in the Islamic East, it found a warm welcome in *al-Andalus* in the Islamic West. As a result, Islamic philosophy flourished in Muslim Spain during the twelfth century. This was largely due to the efforts of great European Muslim philosophers like Ibn Bajjah, known in the Latin West as Avempace, and Ibn Rushd (Averroes). But it was in the works of Ibn Tufayl that Islamic philosophy found a refreshing, innovative and powerful expression. This then exerted considerable influence on European thought and culture.

Muhammad ibn Abd al-Malik ibn Muhammad ibn Tufayl, known as Abubacer in the Western world, was born at Guadix (in present-day Wadi Ash) in Islamic Granada. About a decade before his birth, Granada was occupied by *al-Murabitun* (the al-Moravids). They were a North African dynasty which gained control of Spain in 1086 CE, after more than half a century of political chaos and social unrest in that country. The al-Moravids were founded by the charismatic North African Islamic leader Yusuf ibn Tashfin. They were, at the time, urged by the Muslim world's most important scholars to move into Islamic Spain and restore peace and security there. By the time Ibn Tufayl was born, the al-Moravids had reunited the entire country under their leadership and established much-needed peace and prosperity there.

During this period of stability, young Ibn Tufayl completed his early education in Arabic, the Qur'an and traditional Islamic sciences, before pursuing mathematics, medicine, literature and philosophy. He received advanced training in these subjects at Cordova, Seville and most probably at Toledo, which at the time was one of the most famous centres of learning and scholarship in Islamic Spain. As a student genius, Ibn Tufayl excelled in both the scientific and philosophical sciences and received instant recognition for his mastery of mathematics, medicine and philosophy.

During this period, he also became highly skilled in the philosophical works of Ibn Bajjah, who is widely considered to be the founding father of Andalusian philosophy. A strong rationalistic thinker, Ibn Bajjah attempted to revive and popularise the philosophical thought of great Muslim thinkers like al-Farabi in the Islamic West.

Although Ibn Tufayl disagreed with many parts of Ibn Bajjah's philosophy, he was still heavily influenced by the latter's ideas and thoughts. To a great extent, he is considered to be a natural successor of Ibn Bajjah. The philosophical sciences aside, Ibn Tufayl also excelled in medicine and surgery. Indeed, he was such a popular medical doctor that he established his clinic, despite the declining political situation in Granada.

Following the death of the al-Moravid ruler Ali ibn Yusuf in 1143 CE, political chaos and social unrest again returned to Islamic Spain. This encouraged the neighbouring Christian territories to reorganise their forces and launch fresh attacks into the Islamic regions. In the middle of the chaos there suddenly appeared another powerful Islamic dynasty in North Africa. It was founded originally by Muhammad ibn Tumart (b. 1077-d. 1130 CE). He was a charismatic North African Islamic reformer. The *al-Muwahhidun* (al-Mohads) dynasty carved out a vast empire under the able leadership of Abd al-Mu'min (b. 1094-d. 1163 CE), who moved swiftly to establish his rule across all the territories which were once ruled by the al-Moravids. At the time, Ibn Tufayl was in his late forties and busy practising medicine in Granada.

But, after Yusuf al-Mansur (b. 1135-d. 1184 CE) ascended the al-Mohad throne, he came to hear about Ibn Tufayl's skills as a medical practitioner and arranged for him to be brought to the al-Moravid court. Yusuf al-Mansur was educated in Arabic literature and poetry at Seville. He was a wise and learned ruler who encouraged intellectual and literary pursuits at his luxurious court in Marrakesh. Indeed, he even recruited some of the best Andalusian writers, poets and philosophers to his court. Ibn Tufayl was one such intellectual who served him as a physician, secretary and advisor. The two men became such good friends that they frequently engaged in lengthy discussions on the finer points of philosophy, theology and literature.

Like Yusuf al-Mansur, Ibn Tufayl was also in the habit of recruiting some of the best scholars and thinkers of the time to the court in Marrakesh. One of Ibn Tufayl's star recruits was Ibn Rushd. He was born in 1126 CE into a respectable family of Islamic scholars and jurists in Cordova. Ibn Rushd (see chapter 60) was an outstanding Islamic scholar blessed with an amazing intellect. Although he was much younger than Ibn Tufayl, he became very popular throughout Cordova for his philosophical abilities. This prompted Ibn Tufayl to bring this rising star to the court in Marrakesh. On his arrival at the court, the al-Mohad ruler Yusuf al-Mansur questioned the young philosopher concerning the nature of creation asking him whether he believed in the eternity of the universe.

As Ibn Rushd hesitated to respond, the experienced Ibn Tufayl intervened and answered the monarch's question in a philosophically neutral way. Whether the universe was eternal, or a limited creation of Allah, was a controversial philosophical point, which was hotly debated by Muslim philosophers and theologians alike. The al-Mohads strongly rejected the idea of the eternity of creation. They supported Ghazali's view that the universe was a creation of Allah. Young Ibn Rushd hesitated to answer Yusuf al-Mansur's question, but Ibn Tufayl's timely interruption saved the day for him. Later, the al-Mohad ruler conducted extensive philosophical discussions with Ibn Rushd and expressed his satisfaction with the young philosopher, whom he considered to be both gifted and scholarly. He then rewarded him with a high-ranking government post, working under Ibn Tufayl's supervision.

During this period, Ibn Tufayl not only became Ibn Rushd's mentor and guide but, also helped him to polish his understanding of the finer points of Islamic philosophy and theology. In addition to this, he encouraged Ibn Rushd to write his famous commentaries on the works of Aristotle, which later earned him the popular title of 'The Commentator' throughout the Western world. Unlike Ibn Bajjah, Ibn Tufayl was not a pure rationalist, nor did he subscribe to the philosophical theology of al-Ghazali, even though he was very familiar with both points of view.

As a philosopher, Ibn Bajjah emphasised the importance of rationalism in understanding the nature of creation as well as the attainment of individual 'spiritual' fulfilment. He claimed spiritual fulfilment was achievable intellectually without the need for sensual experience. However influential Sufis like al-Ghazali disagreed with this view. They argued that spiritual success achieved through 'mystical experience' was far superior to the spirituality acquired through rational means. Ibn Tufayl was fully aware of this philosophical/theological clash. He therefore adopted a philosophical position which tried to harmonise these two conflicting views. The philosophical mixture he formulated between the peripatetic thought of al-Farabi and Ibn Sina on the one hand, and al-Ghazali's mystical philosophy on the other, found its most thoughtful expression in his world-famous novel *Risalah Hayy ibn Yaqdhan* (The Tale of Living Son of Vigilant).

Perhaps motivated by Ibn Sina's book of the same title, in this original fictional story Ibn Tufayl explained how a child born on a desert island (located in the Indian Ocean) slowly acquired new skills, improved his knowledge and gained experience to adapt to his new environment. As he grew older and matured, his understanding of life, its meaning and purpose, increased until he was able to think and reason philosophically before going on to experience mystical union, which is the highest spiritual position achievable in Sufism. Later, he met a group of people who lived on a neighbouring island and discovered that they lived by a revealed religious code. His communication with them enabled him to understand and appreciate the true nature and purpose of *wahy* (Divine revelation). But when he attempted to explain to the locals the full meaning and significance of Divine revelation, they showed little interest in learning such knowledge.

Their lack of interest in such matters eventually convinced him that everyone was not necessarily the same. The majority of people were happy to lead ordinary lives. The others, like himself, were very keen on learning philosophical matters to develop a better understanding of life and creation. Before leaving the island, he recommended that the people who wished to lead their lives by following the laws of their religion should be allowed to do so, without being forced to engage in any form of philosophical discussion. He returned to his island, convinced that respect, tolerance and understanding were the keys to survival and co-existence in this hugely diverse world.

Through the life of this fictional character, Ibn Tufayl tried to explain that the *zahiri* (external) way of the ordinary believer was as valid as the *batini* (internal) path of the Sufis. In other words, all the believers, regardless of whether they worshipped in mosques, *zawiyah* (lodges) or sanctuaries, were, in his opinion, seeking the One and the same *Haqq* (truth). Even al-Ghazali acknowledged this fact when he said that the philosophers were also seekers of truth, although only unintentionally. In short, Ibn Tufayl believed that in reality, there was no conflict between *aql* (reason) and *wahy* (revelation). Thus, in his *Risalah*, he attempted to bring together some of the most complex philosophical, mystical and theological disagreements which had been taking place in the Muslim world for many centuries.

Although written in the twelfth century, this original philosophical novel later inspired generations of famous Western thinkers and writers such as Miguel de Cervantes, Baltasar Gracian, Geoffrey Chaucer and Simon Ockley who copied his unique literary style and did so without admitting their main source of inspiration.

This was most certainly the case with the great French philosopher Jean-Jacques Rousseau, who was inspired to pen his 'Emile, or On Education', by Ibn Tufayl's *Risalah*. The same was true of John Locke whose 'An Essay Concerning Human Understanding' and 'A Letter Concerning Toleration' were heavily influenced by Ibn Tufayl's philosophical ideas. But how? His teacher and mentor at the University of Oxford was none other than Edward Pococke who had translated and published a Latin version of the *Risalah* under the title of 'The Self-taught Philosopher' along with the original Arabic text in 1671 CE.

The *Risalah* was also translated into Hebrew in 1349 CE by Moses ben Joshua of Narbonne, thus influencing many of Jewish and Christian theologians and philosophers of the Middle Ages. This book was then translated into English, Dutch, Russian, Spanish, German and other Western languages. Soon it became so popular in Europe that, during the European Enlightenment, it inspired Daniel Defoe (b. 1660-d. 1731 CE) to pen his famous novel Robinson Crusoe in 1719 CE. In addition to the *Risalah*, Ibn Tufayl composed many other essays on philosophical, astronomical and medical topics.

Indeed, as an outstanding astronomer, he helped his student Nur al-Din al-Bitruji (d. 1204 CE), better known as Alpetragius in the Latin West, to review Greek astronomy, including the writings of Ptolemy. After serving as a royal physician to Abu Yaqub Yusuf for nearly two decades, Ibn Tufayl finally retired from government services in 1182 CE. Ibn Rushd, his student and fellow, replaced him as a physician to the al-Mohad ruler. Three years later, this great European Muslim philosopher and writer died at the age of eighty-four and was buried in Marrakesh, in Morocco.

59

Nur al-Din Zangi
(b.1118 - d.1178 CE) /
(b.511 - d.570 AH)

After four hundred years of matchless political supremacy and military domination of the Middle East, the Muslims became politically disunited during the eleventh century. Up until now, the Abbasids had ruled the Islamic world without much opposition. But by the middle of the eleventh century, the Abbasid Empire had become fragmented into several regions. Thus, like the Seljuks, the Buwayhids (or Buyids) became a separate, independent political power at the time. If the political situation in the Islamic East was bad, then the situation in the Islamic West was equally gloomy. After the Umayyad rule of Islamic Spain abruptly ended in 1031 CE, political chaos became normal in that part of the world. This prompted the energised European nations to flex their muscles and reassert their political authority in and around the Mediterranean Sea, pushing the Muslims back further into the East.

Although the rise of the Seljuk dynasty did bring in a period of peace and prosperity for a time, after the death of the Seljuk ruler Malik Shah in 1092 CE, this dynasty also began to decline rapidly. As political rivalry and social chaos spread across much of the Muslim world, the Crusaders entered the Muslim sphere of influence in 1096 CE. They established a Crusader Kingdom in

Palestine. After capturing Jerusalem, Islam's third holiest city, the Crusaders threatened to overpower the entire Islamic East. Then Sultan Nur al-Din Zangi, the famous Saint-King of the Zangid dynasty, emerged to rally the Muslim world to confront the Crusaders for the first time.

Mahmud Zangi, known as Nur al-Din Zangi for short, was born in the northern Iraqi city of Mosul. His father, Imad al-Din Zangi (b. 1087-d. 1146 CE), was a Turkish military commander who was in the service of the Seljuks. As an able military commander and teacher of the Sultan's two sons, Imad al-Din led a privileged lifestyle surrounded by much wealth and luxury. Young Nur al-Din was therefore brought up and educated in his father's luxurious and secluded mansion in Mosul. Being learned, Imad al-Din ensured his son received a thorough education in Arabic and the Islamic sciences. Young Nur al-Din was known to be very pious during his early years. In 1127 CE, when Nur al-Din was only ten, the Seljuk ruler Sultan Mahmud II appointed Imad al-Din as governor of Mosul. This prompted Imad to take pre-strategic actions to stop the decline of Islamic political power and military might.

As a gifted planner and military commander, Imad al-Din could see the signs of weakness within the Seljuk administration – and across the Islamic East – and he was determined to stop the rot. Thus, soon after becoming governor, he declared his independence from the Seljuks and established a separate political entity consisting of the cities of Sinjar, Nasibin, Harran and others, with his political headquarters based in Mosul.

A year later, he took advantage of the chaos in Aleppo at the time and added that city to his expanding empire. He then seized the territories of Hamah and Hims but, to his huge disappointment, he failed to capture the historic city of Damascus. As soon as Imad al-Din began to flex his muscles, the rulers of Damascus and the Crusader Kingdom in Palestine felt threatened by his growing power. This prompted them to unite against him. Not willing to fight on two fronts simultaneously, Imad turned his attention towards Edessa, the capital of the oldest Crusader State in the Muslim world. The capture of this city by the Muslims under the leadership of Imad al-Din in 1144 CE sent a shockwave through the ranks of the Crusaders. It also revived the Muslims' determination to drive out the Crusaders from the Islamic East.

The fall of Edessa was a truly historic event. It marked the beginning of the end of the Crusader presence in the Muslim world, and the first major victory of Islam over its Frankish enemy. Two years after the capture of Edessa, Imad al-Din was murdered by his bodyguard in 1146 CE. As the news of his death spread across the Zangid kingdom, chaos and confusion followed until Nur al-Din, his second son, emerged to restore peace and order across the region.

Tall, slim, dark-skinned, bearded and equally charming and gentle, Nur al-Din succeeded his father as the Sultan of the Zangid kingdom at the age of twenty-nine. Like his father, Nur al-Din was a brave, intelligent and learned ruler. However, unlike his father, he was a devout Muslim whose piety and virtues turned him into a mighty symbol of Islamic goodness and righteousness. As a ruler and statesman, the Sultan was determined to reunite the Muslim world under the banner of Islam and drive out the Crusaders from the Islamic East. Although the liberation of Jerusalem from the grip of its Frankish invaders was one of his top long-term objectives, immediately upon becoming Sultan his priority was to establish his political authority across the Zangid Kingdom.

After appointing his brother, Sayf al-Din, governor of Mosul and its surrounding territories, he moved to Aleppo to take care of that strategically important principality. On his arrival in Syria, he received news that Edessa had again fallen into the hands of the enemy. Determined not to allow Edessa to remain in the hands of the Crusaders for long, for that would have sent the wrong message and undermined Muslim morale, he organised a force and marched to Edessa at lightning speed. He arrived there even before the Crusaders could organise their defences properly. Seeing him marching on Edessa with a large army prompted the Crusaders to flee, leaving the city in the hands of the brave Nur al-Din. The recapture of Edessa without a fight won him widespread praise and helped to secure his position as the supreme ruler of the Zangid dynasty.

From a strategic point of view, the Sultan's political power and authority was further strengthened by the instigators of the second Crusade who, instead of taking Edessa or Aleppo, foolishly attacked Damascus whose ruler, Mu'in al-Din Unar, was the only Muslim ruler to have allied himself with the Crusader Kingdom in Palestine. However, the Crusaders' siege of Damascus backfired spectacularly when Mu'in al-Din's forces inflicted a crushing defeat on the powerful Frankish army. A year after the Franks' humiliating defeat at the Battle of Damascus (1148 CE), Mu'in al-Din died. This left the door wide open for Sultan Nur al-Din to move in and further expand his empire. As expected, the Sultan captured Antioch and five years later added Damascus to his expanding empire. As a seasoned politician, he captured both of these cities through a combination of diplomacy and limited warfare. He was inspired by his determination to reclaim Jerusalem from the Crusaders. So Nur al-Din now became a powerful rival of the Crusader kingdom.

Soon his call for *jihad* (armed struggle) against the Crusaders began to echo across the Islamic East. This call won the thirty-seven-year-old monarch much-needed support and recognition across the Muslim world. With Jerusalem now very much within his reach, his dream of liberating Islam's third holiest site from the grip of the Crusaders seemed a real possibility. But his plans were ruined by a powerful earthquake which struck Syria in 1157 CE and completely devastated the country. In the same year, he fell seriously ill. Confined to his bed for a year and a half, Ibn al-Waqqar, his physician, did not expect him to survive but, thanks to his resolve, he eventually made a full recovery.

Again, as the Sultan contemplated the possibility of taking the fight to the Crusaders in Jerusalem, he received news of Byzantine military activity to the north of Syria. When he contacted the Byzantine Emperor Manuel I, he assured Nur al-Din that he had no intention of attacking Zangid territories. But still, the presence of Byzantine forces close to his borders prevented the Sultan from launching an attack against the Franks. Most unexpectedly, during this period, Egypt rather than Palestine became the main theatre of warfare. Indeed, the Sultan's forces played a central role in reclaiming this strategically important country from the Fatimids. After Egypt became a Fatimid stronghold during the tenth century, it was ruled by a succession of Caliphs who saw themselves as rivals of the Abbasid Caliphs in Baghdad. But, by the middle of the twelfth century, the Fatimid grip on Egypt had become very shaky. So much so that from 1163 to 1169 CE, the Fatimids clashed with the Franks and the Zangids on more than one occasion over the rich prize that was Egypt.

At the insistence of his gifted general Asad al-Din Shirkuh, the uncle of the famous Salah al-Din (Saladin), Sultan Nur al-Din eventually authorised a large-scale military mission against Egypt to add this country to his empire. As a result, three determined fighters clashed with each other to gain control of Egypt. They were Shawar, an Egyptian Minister who seized power in Cairo in 1162 CE and ruled the country with an iron fist. Amalric was a Frankish ruler who was eager to capture this strategically important Muslim country. The third was Shirkuh, the Kurdish general in the service of Sultan Nur al-Din. These three men fought each other for nearly a decade to gain control of Egypt until Shirkuh, assisted by his young nephew Salah al-Din, finally triumphed in 1169 CE. His victory enabled Nur al-Din to add Egypt to his expanding empire. However, after Shirkuh's unexpected death, young Salah al-Din exercised power in Egypt on behalf of Sultan Nur al-Din. Although Salah al-Din remained loyal to the Sultan, in reality, he came to be seen as an independent ruler in his own right.

As time passed, Sultan Nur al-Din's dream of reclaiming Jerusalem from the grip of the Crusaders began to slowly fade away. He became confined to his bed from an angina attack; his health was now deteriorating rapidly. When his doctors wanted to operate on him, he refused to permit them, saying that nature should take its course. Though he was unable to liberate Islam's third holiest city from the Crusaders, the credit for unifying the Islamic East must go to Sultan Nur al-Din. More importantly, he paved the way for Salah al-Din to take the fight to the Crusaders and re-establish Islamic political authority across the region.

As a remarkably loyal Muslim, he was very eager to see the flag of Islam flying high over Jerusalem and the rest of the Muslim world. By all accounts, he was a just, pious and generous ruler who possessed a truly sublime character and personality. Not surprisingly, renowned historians like ibn al-Athir, Ibn Khallikan and ibn al-Jawzi have lavished much praise on him, often referring to him as the 'Saint-King' of Islam.

Indeed, according to Ibn al-Athir, when the Sultan's wife once complained to him that she had insufficient money to meet their family's needs, he told her she could not have any more, as all the money kept at the *bait al-mal* (public treasury) belonged to the public. He was not prepared, he said, to throw himself into the fire by wrongfully consuming public money. Also, being very learned, he loved the company of the *ulama* (religious scholars) and rejected materialistic values and practices. He encouraged his officials to serve the public with honesty, dedication and care. He led such an exemplary lifestyle that even a brave and stubborn Salah al-Din never dared to cross his path. When Ayyub, the father of Salah al-Din, was once informed that his son wished to break his contract with Sultan Nur al-Din, he told his son categorically that he would never tolerate any form of disobedience or disloyalty to the master of Aleppo. Ayyub's devotion to Sultan Nur al-Din may have surprised Salah al-Din, but it certainly did not surprise those who knew their master well.

Referring to Sultan Nur al-Din, the historian Ibn al-Athir wrote, 'I have studied the careers of the rulers of the past but, apart from the first four Caliphs and Umar ibn Abd al-Aziz, there has been no prince so liberal and pious, law-abiding and just (as Nur al-Din).' Sultan Nur al-Din Mahmud Zangi, the famous 'Saint-King' of Islam, passed away at the age of fifty-six and was buried in Damascus.

The news of his death came like a thunderbolt from the heavens and the people of Syria crammed into the mosques to pray for his soul. The son of Zangi continues to live in our memories to this day, for he was a true *mujahid* (warrior), who devoted his entire life to the service of Islam. Is it any wonder then that today young children grow up across the Muslim world listening to stories about the virtues, heroic deeds and achievements of the son of Zangi.

60

Ibn Rushd
(b.1126 - d.1198 CE) /
(b.520 - d.595 AH)

When Tariq ibn Ziyad (see chapter 18) crossed the sea and landed in Gibraltar in 711 CE, he found Europeans were still living in the Dark Ages. His expedition into Spain thus represented a new dawn for Europe as a whole. For nearly eight centuries, the Muslims of *al-Andalus* (or Islamic Spain) became the creators of a new European civilisation and captured the imagination of all of Europe with their incredible contributions in all areas of human work. And so, the light of civility and civilisation – lit by the Muslims of Spain – continued to burn fiercely across Europe, right up until the modern period.

Through Islamic Spain, Muslims not only introduced Plato, Aristotle, Algebra and papermaking to Europe, they also built magnificent works of art and architecture and established some of Europe's first schools, colleges, libraries and hospitals. Moreover, it was during this period that the Spanish roads and streets became some of Europe's first to be lit by lamps, thanks once again to the Muslims. It should also be pointed out that it was the Spanish Muslims who played a central role in the development and cultivation of the European mind.

Thus, great European Muslim philosophers and thinkers like Ibn Hazm (see chapter 53), Ibn Massarrah, Ibn Bajjah, Ibn Tufayl (see chapter 58) and Ibn al-Arabi (see chapter 65) blazed a trail which captured the European imagination like never before. These remarkable philosophers and thinkers were not only Muslims; they were also some of medieval Europe's most influential intellectuals and writers. However, one man had more influence on medieval European philosophy and thought than probably any other. He was none other than Ibn Rushd.

Muhammad ibn Ahmad ibn Muhammad ibn Rushd, known in the Western world as Averroes, was born in Cordova, the capital of Muslim Spain. At the time it was one of the most famous centres of learning and higher education in Europe. He was born into a distinguished Muslim family of educationalists, judges and intellectuals who occupied senior governmental positions in Spain. Ibn Rushd's grandfather, Muhammad, was a respected authority on *fiqh* (Islamic jurisprudence) and served as an imam of the Grand Mosque in Cordova. His father, Ahmad, was the leading Islamic scholar of his generation, who served as *qadi* (judge) of Cordova and acquired a considerable reputation for his deep knowledge of traditional Islamic sciences. During his early years, Ibn Rushd studied Arabic, the Qur'an and *fiqh* under his father's guidance, as well as *hadith* (Prophetic traditions) and *usul al-hadith* (science of *Hadith*). Ibn Rushd then received advanced training in Islamic jurisprudence and mastered *Maliki* legal thought.

As a gifted student, he excelled in *Maliki fiqh*, and pursued higher education in scientific and philosophical sciences including astronomy, mathematics, philosophy, logic, medicine and history. Being the only great Muslim philosopher to have been an expert on comparative fiqh, he later became famous for his grasp of *ikhtilaf* (juristic differences). He served in the capacity of judge and lawyer for many years. Known to have been very hardworking and industrious, he used to read for up to sixteen hours a day and did so even when he was in his late sixties. He was also familiar with both Greek and Hebrew.

Ibn Rushd lived in a politically volatile period in the history of Islamic Spain. After the Umayyad rule of Spain came to an end in 1031, political in-fighting and ethnic rivalry broke out until the Moroccan-based *al-Murabitun* (al-Moravids) marched into Spain under the able leadership of Yusuf ibn Tashfin and reunited the warring factions. In 1146 CE, when Ibn Rushd was only twenty, the al-Moravids were overthrown by the *al-Muwahhidun* (al-Mohads), another powerful political and religious movement, which was founded in Morocco. They went on to rule Islamic Spain for nearly a century. Despite the unpredictable socio-political circumstances of the time, Ibn Rushd continued to serve the interests of the Muslims by remaining loyal to the al-Mohads, although he also had close family ties with the al-Moravids.

This was indeed a tricky balancing act for him, especially because the al-Mohads had received only a halfhearted reception from the people of *al-Andalus*. In the circumstances, his decision to serve the new rulers was a courageous act rather than an opportunistic one because he could have chosen to move to Morocco if he wished. Indeed, his old friend Ibn Tufayl, whom he had met at Abu Yaqub Yusuf's (b. 1135-d. 1184 CE) court in Seville, did just that. As the governor's personal physician, Ibn Tufayl wielded considerable political power and it was on his recommendation that Ibn Rushd came to enjoy the governor's support after he became the Caliph of Muslim Spain.

Soon after becoming Caliph, Abu Yaqub Yusuf transferred the capital of Islamic Spain to Seville and appointed Ibn Rushd a *qadi* (judge). Deeply impressed by his profound knowledge of Islamic jurisprudence, medicine and philosophy, the Caliph promoted him to the highest position within his courts. As a devout Muslim and competent judge, he was a firm believer in the principles of justice, fairness and equality. He sought to uphold the *Sharia* (Divine law)and render justice irrespective of one's race, colour, creed or position. His profound knowledge of Islamic law, combined with his qualities of honesty, fair play and neutrality in legal matters, soon won him much praise and endeared him to Caliph Abu Yaqub Yusuf. As a qadi, Ibn Rushd not only discharged his legal duties with honesty, efficiency and effectiveness but also engaged in advanced research in aspects of law, philosophy and science during his spare time.

Although he wrote numerous books on Islamic jurisprudence, his *Bidayat al-Mujtahid wa Nihayat al-Muqtasid* (An Opening for Those Who Exert and an End for the Contented) is widely considered to be a brilliant contribution to the field of Islamic jurisprudence. In this book he argued that diversity in *ikhtilaf* (the interpretation of law) did not entail distortion of the truth; rather it is another way of reaching the truth in its broadest sense. *Ikhtilaf* therefore represented a method rather than a barrier to the attainment of a better understanding of the spirit of the Divine law.

Ibn Rushd's Bidayat is an extremely important work on Islamic legal thought which continues to be read and widely consulted by Islamic jurists to this day. Ibn Rushd's achievements in Islamic jurisprudence were considerable. His contributions to science and philosophy were nothing short of remarkable. In addition to studying astronomy and mathematics, he excelled in medicine and, after Ibn Tufayl's retirement, Caliph Abu Yaqub Yusuf called Ibn Rushd to Marrakesh and appointed him to be his personal physician. Ibn Tufayl was a renowned physician of his time who had served the Caliph with great distinction but Abu Yaqub Yusuf's decision to appoint Ibn Rushd as his personal physician says a lot about Ibn Rushd's skills and abilities as a medical practitioner.

As it happens, his decades of research in medical science, combined with many years of professional experience as a physician, earned him widespread recognition across Cordova as a respected authority on medicine. He was familiar with the medical thought of both Galen and Ibn Sina. He attempted to combine ancient Greek medical thought with Islamic medical practices to develop an original synthesis of the two schools.

He wrote more than twenty essays on all aspects of medicine, including his famous, 'The Book of Universal Rules of Medicine', which was a medical encyclopaedia written at the request of Caliph Abu Yaqub Yusuf. In this book, he explained the fundamental principles and practices of medicine from a rationalistic point of view. By adopting such a rationalistic approach to medicine, he sought to move from the physical to the rational dimension to develop a new combination between Galenic thought and Islamic medicine. Ibn Rushd's approach to medicine was not only sophisticated, but it was also holistic and very refreshing.

He continued to serve Caliph Abu Yaqub Yusuf – and then his son and successor Abu Yusuf 'al-Mansur' – as a personal physician until in 1194 CE, when at the age of around sixty-eight, he was ordered by the Caliph to leave Marrakesh to please the conservative *ulama* (religious scholars). They considered Ibn Rushd's philosophical and theological ideas to be unorthodox and heretical. During this period, his books were publicly burnt by the conservative *ulama* and a huge public outcry broke out across the city. This forced the Caliph to restrict the teaching of philosophy and other rational sciences for a while. Later, the Caliph recalled Ibn Rushd to Marrakesh where he continued to write and pursue research in philosophy, theology and medicine.

As an encyclopaedic genius of the highest order, Ibn Rushd did not believe in the compartmentalisation of knowledge and, therefore, he refused to confine himself to one subject alone. In addition to being an eminent jurist, a distinguished physician and an outstanding theologian, he was also one of the greatest Muslim philosophers of all time. Since his breadth of learning was colossal, his approach to *kalam* (theology) and *falsafah* (philosophy) was both sophisticated and analytical.

Unfortunately, his critics failed to understand and appreciate the sheer scope and intensity of his religious thought and scholarship. Blessed with an unusually sharp and penetrating mind, he acquired an unrivalled mastery of Islamic thought and worldview. His ability to delve deep into the finer points of Islamic theology, philosophy and jurisprudence — whether to prove, offer a fresh interpretation or reject a specific thought — was nothing short of breathtaking. If an Islamic intellectual of Ibn Taymiyyah's level struggled to understand the complexity of Ibn Rushd's ideas and thoughts, it is not surprising that the ordinary people on the streets of Cordova failed to grasp the details of his interpretations.

Some of Ibn Rushd's major theological and philosophical works include, 'The Decisive Treatise on the Nature of the Connection between Philosophy and Religion', 'Revelation of Methods of Proofs concerning the Beliefs of the Nation' and 'Refutation of the Refutation'. These three books were written in Seville on his return from Morocco. As a devout student of the Qur'an, in these works, he argued that the Qur'an not only encouraged Muslims to think, ponder and contemplate but also to utilise their rational faculties to acquire a better understanding of creation and physical phenomena in general.

According to Ibn Rushd, there was no conflict between reason and revelation, and therefore religion and philosophy were not incompatible in Islam. Imam al-Ghazali strongly criticiszed his philosophy in his book, 'The Refutation of Philosophers'. In this celebrated book, al-Ghazali accused the philosophers of heresy. But Ibn Rushd rejected his views and defended the thoughts of the philosophers with great wit and eloquence. Ibn Rushd accepted that religion based on revelation was far superior to a purely rational approach to religion. But, he passionately disagreed with those who argued that reason had no role to play in religion. Ibn Rushd championed a form of religious rationalism which tried to merge religion with philosophy, and faith with reason.

Furthermore, he argued that the study of philosophy was not a blameworthy activity; rather it was an important and admirable pursuit. Indeed, according to Ibn Rushd, from an Islamic legal perspective, the study of philosophy could be classified as a recommended occupation. However, his critics refused to accept his philosophical interpretation of Islam because he was heavily influenced by Aristotle. His religious rationalism, they argued, represented nothing more than the Aristotelianiszation of Islam. Though Ibn Rushd was undoubtedly influenced by Aristotle's philosophy and thought, his critics were wrong to accuse him of promoting a form of Islamic Aristotelianism. The truth was, he was too good an intellectual to engage in such an intellectually rebellious activity. He also repeatedly pointed out that his critics had failed to understand his rationalistic approach to religion, and thus their charge of heresy levelled against him was unfair and unjustified.

In addition to numerous works on philosophy, law and medicine, Ibn Rushd published scores of books on logic, astronomy, physics and cosmology. According to some historians he composed as many as seventy major works. Also, his mastery of Greek philosophy and extensive commentaries on the major works of Aristotle later earned him the popular title of 'The Commentator'. He was considered to be Europe's greatest authority on Aristotle. His commentaries were read and studied widely. He was also respected throughout medieval Europe as a philosopher par excellence. His ideas and thoughts inspired both Jewish and Christian thinkers alike. So much so that two different schools of thought subsequently emerged in Europe, namely 'Jewish Averroists' and 'Christian Averroists'.

The famous Italian poet Dante Alighieri rated him highly. In his acclaimed book, he mentioned two great Muslim philosophers by name, Ibn Sina (Avicenna) and Ibn Rushd (Averroes), both of them had tremendous influence on all the great medieval and modern European scholars and thinkers, including St. Thomas Aquinas Albert the Great, Maimonides, Roger Bacon, John Locke, Blaise Pascal and Immanuel Kant.

Ibn Rushd acquired a large following in Europe so his followers later became known as the 'Latin Averroists'. His works were passionately studied at universities across Europe including Avignon, Paris, Padua, Bologna and Naples, among others. He was accused in the Islamic East for his supposed heresy but Ibn Rushd became an intellectual pioneer in medieval Europe. Thus he paved the way for the Renaissance. After a lifetime devoted to the pursuit of knowledge and wisdom, Ibn Rushd, the great European Muslim theologian, jurist, physician and philosopher, died in Marrakesh (in present-day Morocco) at the age of seventy-two. Later, his remains were transferred to his native Cordova, where a statue has been erected in his honour.

61

Salah al-Din Ayyubi (b.1138 - d.1193 CE) / (b.533 - d.589 AH)

The 12th century was one of the most difficult and chaotic periods in Muslim history. The unity of the Muslim *ummah* (global Muslim community) was shattered by constant political and internal conflict. In the Islamic East, the once awesome Abbasid Caliphate and the Seljuk Dynasty became politically weak and were in power only in name. The same was true of the once powerful Fatimid kingdom of Egypt. In addition, the territories of the Islamic Fertile Crescent became divided and subdivided into tiny territories. Their rulers frequently fought each other for political and military domination. To make matters worse, at the same time, the Muslims also came under direct threat from a tough foreign enemy, namely the Crusaders who had set out from Europe to conquer the Islamic East.

The Muslims were thus caught unprepared by the Crusaders. They captured a large stretch of Islamic territories on the coast of the Eastern Mediterranean. They then marched towards the biggest prize, *al-quds* or Jerusalem, the third sacred city of Islam. Of course, the bitterly divided Muslim rulers of the time had no answer to the might and firepower Crusaders who inflicted a crushing defeat on them. They captured Jerusalem and massacred its citizens collectively. At a time when the Muslims found themselves hopelessly outplayed by the Crusaders, the legendary Sultan, Salah al-Din emerged to restore the battered pride and prestige of the Muslim *ummah*.

Salah al-Din Yusuf ibn Ayyub, known in the Western world as Saladin, was born in Tikrit in modern Iraq. Of Kurdish origin, his family were originally from the Central Asian country of Armenia. After settling in the territory which now includes northern Iraq, parts of Turkey and Syria, the members of the Ayyub family became prominent citizens of their locality. Both Salah al-Din's father and uncle became distinguished members of Sultan Imad al-Din Zangi's political and civil government. In the year Salah al-Din was born, his father Najm al-Din Ayyub was appointed governor of the ancient city of Heliopolis (Ba'alabek, located in Lebanon). Thus, young Salah al-Din spent his early years in this ancient city. Since his father was a learned individual of Sufi (Islamic spirituality) orientation, he erected a *zawiyah* (Sufi lodge) for his spiritually inclined friends. During his early years, Salah al-Din learned the Qur'an and received thorough training in traditional Islamic sciences, Arabic grammar, literature, and poetry.

Najm al-Din Ayyub's outstanding services to Imad al-Din, the reigning monarch, earned him considerable honour. However, after the sudden death of Imad, Ayyub's family was forced to suffer political and economic hardship. Ayyub was persuaded by his brother, Asad al-Din Shirkuh, to cooperate with the new monarch of the Zangid dynasty by the name of Nur al-Din. Ayyub agreed to help Nur al-Din strengthen his power. Then Nur al-Din rewarded Ayyub for his cooperation by appointing him the governor of Damascus (see chapter 59). At the time Salah al-Din was a teenager and spent the next decade at his father's residence in Damascus. Being the son of the governor, he was held in high esteem by everyone. It is also reported that during this period, Salah al-Din became very fond of the monarch Nur al-Din because of his personal piety and exemplary conduct and behaviour.

Impressed by Nur al-Din's constant devotion to Islamic principles and practices, Salah al-Din also moulded his character and personality by following Islamic teachings. Indeed, his respect for Islamic principles, combined with his perfect habits and sublime qualities, later earned him great commendation both in the East and the West. Even his critics could not help but admire him for his acts of kindness, generosity and tolerance. Salah al-Din disliked pomp and ceremony. He devoted much of his time to daily prayers and other *ibadah* (devotional acts). Like Nur al-Din, he led a simple and austere lifestyle, far removed from the luxuries and material pleasures of this life. Until the age of twenty-five, he led a normal life without showing any signs of the great man that he was to be. Having led an uneventful and relatively calm childhood and early adult life, he expected to pass smoothly into a restful old age. But he suddenly found himself forced into the murky and dangerous world of global politics.

Struck down by a disease, Sultan Nur al-Din was confined to his bed. That is when Shirkuh, the uncle of Salah al-Din and commander-in-chief of Nur al-Din's armed forces, approached the ill Sultan. He asked his permission to launch a military expedition against the traitors who were rulers of the Fatimid Kingdom of Egypt. After some hesitation, the Sultan authorised Shirkuh to lead an expedition against the Fatimids. During this campaign, Shirkuh and his nephew Salah al-Din overcame all their opponents. They took full control of Fatimid Egypt. Soon after capturing Egypt, Shirkuh died without consolidating his power grip on the country. Salah al-Din had come with his uncle reluctantly. So, he was happy to let his experienced uncle make all the important decisions. But now he had no choice. He had to take matters into his own hands and, in doing so, he carved out a unique place for himself in the records of history.

Three days after Shirkuh's death, the Fatimid ruler Caliph al-Adid asked Salah al-Din to succeed his uncle. The Caliph conferred on him the title of *al-Malik an-Nasir* (the Supporting King). He was only thirty at the time. His accession to power in Egypt made him a stronger, more determined and wiser political operator. But he continued to lead a private lifestyle far detached from the joys and pleasures of an aristocratic, rich and noble life. According to his peers, Salah al-Din's personal life remained as simple as ever. He continued to devote long periods to prayer and contemplation. Devout and wise, he also worked tirelessly to unify the Muslim world under the banner of Islam and, in so doing, established a powerful empire in the Islamic East. His main aim was to liberate the sacred city of Jerusalem from the grip of the Crusaders. 'When

Allah Almighty granted me the land of Egypt', Salah al-Din later recalled, 'I was certain that Palestine would also fall to me.'

While Salah al-Din was busy planning to liberate Jerusalem from the Crusaders, the other Muslim rulers were busy fighting each other to increase their personal power and wealth. Then again, gifted men like Salah al-Din are not born every day; rather they emerge during critical times in human history and, by the sheer force of their character and personality, they change the course of world history. After becoming the ruler of Egypt, his main political objective was to restore the honour of Islam by driving out the Crusaders from Islamic Jerusalem. His unexpected success against the Crusaders firmly established his reputation as a great champion of Islam. He also became one of the most successful warrior-kings in the annals of history.

As al-Malik al-Nasir, Salah al-Din instigated wide-ranging reforms within the highest ranks of power in Egypt. He reshuffled the civil and administrative structures of his government. He removed most of the corrupt, scheming and treacherous elements from his administration and replaced them with clean, honest and upright people. He then sent an invitation to his father, Ayyub, who at the time was living in Damascus, to join him in Egypt. Ayyub migrated to Egypt with his entire family, including his distant relatives and acquaintances. Salah al-Din was now surrounded for the first time by his close family members and friends. At last, he became the undisputed ruler of Egypt. Needless to say, the consolidation of his grip on power in Egypt helped him to carry out further reforms. He abolished the corrupt Fatimid dynasty and redistributed all the wealth and properties the Fatimids had accumulated.

He divided this wealth into three portions. He sent a share to the Abbasid Caliph in Baghdad. Another portion to Damascus for Sultan Nur al-Din. The remainder was deposited in the bait *al-mal* (public treasury) for the welfare of the Egyptian people. Salah al-Din refused to keep anything for himself or his family. His kindness and generosity soon endeared him to the public as he lavished them with gifts and presents while preferring to live a very simple and austere lifestyle himself. Indeed, he refused to live in the pompous and extravagant Caliphal palaces built by the Fatimids, choosing instead to live in his old and dated residence in Cairo. When this residence eventually became too small for the smooth and effective operation of his government, he built himself a simple but elegant building in Cairo so that he could perform his duties as the ruler of Egypt with efficiency and effectiveness.

Soon after consolidating his power in Egypt, Salah al-Din received the news of Sultan Nur al-Din's death in 1174 CE. He understood the gravity of the situation and moved swiftly to avoid any internal conflict in Syria. By doing this he assumed full control of that strategically important country. Following his capture of Syria, he appointed his nephew, Farooq Shah, to be the governor of that territory. Still only thirty-six, Salah al-Din now embarked on a series of military campaigns to strengthen and unify the warring neighbouring Muslim lands. In addition to Syria and Mesopotamia, he successfully captured a large part of North Africa including Tunisia, Libya and much of Arabia as well as Yemen. Salah al-Din soon carved out a huge empire and became the undisputed leader of the Muslim world at the time.

As one of the most powerful Muslim rulers of his time, Salah al-Din could have chosen to spend the rest of his life in peace and comfort if he wished. Instead, he focused his attention on the rebellious activities of the Crusaders who, at the time, maintained a tight grip on Palestine. After establishing themselves in that country, the Crusaders began to wreak havoc throughout the entire region. So much so, that on one occasion they marched very close to Madinah, the city of the Prophet. They threatened to overwhelm the city. When Salah al-Din received news of the Crusaders' outrageous behaviour towards the people of Madinah, he vowed to punish the culprits with his own hands. As commander-in-chief of the armed forces, he left Egypt and marched with his army towards Palestine to confront the threat of the Crusaders.

He came face to face with the opponents at a place called Tiberias, near the Sea of Galilee. A fierce clash followed. His troops launched such a vicious and coordinated attack on the Franks (western European people) that soon the latter began to lose heart. In desperation, some Frankish generals abandoned their forces and came directly to Salah al-Din. They pleaded with him to speed up his victory to ease their pain and agony. During this historic encounter, known as the Battle of Hittin, Salah al-Din also taught the Frankish Crusaders a good lesson in kindness, generosity and compassion. From that day on, his name became a symbol of bravery and heroism both in the East and the West.

Victory at Tiberias opened the door to the rest of Palestine. He moved swiftly before the Franks could regroup again. Salah al-Din was able to offer his Friday congregational prayer inside the same mosque which had been converted into a church three generations earlier by the Crusaders. Salah al-Din single-handedly took on the combined might of Europe and cut it to pieces. It did not take him long to capture the rest of Palestine including, of course, Jerusalem. He did so without shedding any innocent blood. By contrast, when the Crusaders first entered Jerusalem, they put all its inhabitants to the sword. The entire city ran red with blood. But Salah al-Din's acts of kindness, generosity and benevolence won the hearts and minds of all its population. Christian reporters of the Crusades could not help but shower much praise on him for his exemplary behaviour and attitude towards the people of Jerusalem.

Thanks to Salah al-Din, *al-quds* - the third sacred city of Islam - again came under Islamic rule. With his mission accomplished, Salah al-Din returned to Damascus where he built many schools, mosques and hospitals, and passed away around the age of fifty-five. He lies buried in the vicinity of the city's historic Umayyad mosque. His name and fame continue to echo throughout the Muslim world, as well as in the West, to this day. A man of truly remarkable character and sublime qualities, it is not surprising that Salah al-Din is today considered to be one of history's most famous heroes and influential Muslims.

62

Mu'in al-Din Chisti
(b.1143 - d.1236 CE) /
(b.537 - d.634 AH)

All popular Sufi (Islamic spiritual) Orders, like the *qadiriyah*, *naqshbandiyah*, *suhrawardiyah* and *shadhiliyah*, trace their spiritual lineage back to the Prophet through his close companions such as Abu Bakr al-Siddiq (see chapter 3) and Ali ibn Abi Talib (see chapter 8). However, as al-Hujwiri (b. 1009-d. 1077 CE), the eleventh-century Sufi scholar, pointed out in his famous *Kashf al-Mahjub* (Removal of the Veil), that during the early days of Islam, Sufism was a reality without the label. However after the increase of materialistic values and practices in the Islamic world, Sufism became a label without a reality. This state of affairs prompted famous Islamic scholars and Sufis, like al-Hujwiri, to oppose the spread of pleasure-seeking and materialistic values and practices which threatened to overwhelm Islamic societies at the time.

It was a critical period in Islamic history, when the decline in Abbasid political power, coupled with the invasion of foreign intellectual and cultural influences, began to undermine Islamic values, principles and practices. During this challenging period, several influential Sufis, like Abd al-Qadir al-Jilani (see chapter 57), Shihab al-Din al-Suhrawardi, Najm al-Din Kubra and Khwajah Hamdani emerged to champion Islamic morals, religiousness and spirituality. A contemporary of these luminaries was Mu'in al-Din Chishti. He became the founder of the *chishtiyah* Sufi Order in India. Today it is widely considered to be one of the subcontinent's most influential Sufi Orders.

Mu'in al-Din Muhammad ibn Hasan, also known as Aftab-I Mulk-i Hind (the Sun of the Kingdom of India), was born in Sistan into a noble Muslim family. His father, Ghiyath al-Din Hasan, was a relatively successful businessman who also became well-known for his personal piety, worship, religiousness and Sufi tendencies. He was keen to educate his son. Young Mu'in al-Din was enrolled at his local school and received a thorough education in Arabic, Persian and the Islamic sciences. Despite the political uncertainty and social unrest of the times, he completed his elementary and intermediate-level studies. He was barely fifteen when his father suddenly died. This forced his family to endure considerable financial hardship.

Thankfully, Mu'in al-Din had inherited a share of a garden and a water mill from his father. This earned him enough income to pay for his daily expenses. To make matters worse, his beloved mother then passed away, which again forced him to experience more personal and financial hardships. Upset and devastated by his loss, he sold his inheritance and distributed all the proceeds to the poor and the needy.

He then travelled extensively in pursuit of knowledge and wisdom. In addition to Bukhara and Samarqand, he visited many other renowned centres of Islamic learning and studied under the guidance of many prominent scholars and Sufis. During this period, he committed the entire Qur'an to memory and became a talented explainer of traditional Islamic sciences. On his arrival in Harwan, on the outskirts of Nishapur, he encountered Khwajah Uthman Harwani (b. 1107-d. 1220 CE), who was a distinguished Islamic scholar and prominent *chishtiyah* Sufi. Here he became a member of Khwajah Harwani's Sufi circle and spent the next two decades in his company.

Under Khwajah Harwani's guidance, he mastered both the *zahiri* (outer) and *batini* (inner) dimensions of Islam, before travelling with his teacher to Makkah and Madinah to perform the sacred *hajj*. After staying in Harwan, he left Khwajah Harwani's company and travelled to Baghdad, the capital of the Abbasid Caliphate, to receive advanced training in Islamic sciences and Sufism.

During his stay in Baghdad, he met many famous Islamic scholars and Sufis like Abd al-Qadir al-Jilani (the founder of the *qadiriyah* Sufi Order), Shihab al-Din al-Suhrawardi (the founder of the *suhrawardiyah* Sufi Order), as well as Khwajah Yusuf Hamdani and Shaykh al-Tabrizi. Before this, he had also met the legendary Central Asian Sufi sage Najm al-Din Kubra, the founder of the *kubrawiyah* Sufi Order, and studied Islamic spiritual practices under his guidance for around two and a half years. Thanks to his extensive education and training in traditional Islamic sciences and spirituality, Mu'in al-Din soon established his reputation as a master of Sufism and one of its most eloquent explainers.

From Baghdad, he went to Isfahan where he met another famous Sufi sage, Shaykh al-Isfahani, who admired him for his deep understanding of Islamic sciences and spirituality. Here he also met one of his most famous disciples, Khwajah Qutb al-Din Bakhtiyar Kaki (b. 1173-d. 1235 CE). Qutb al-Din originally came to Isfahan to join the company of Shaykh al-Isfahani but when he met Mu'in al-Din he changed his mind and instead pledged allegiance to Mu'in al-Din. He was in his mid-forties when he moved from Isfahan to Ghazna (in present-day Afghanistan). He was accompanied by a handful of disciples he had gathered around him.

On his arrival in Ghazna, Mu'in al-Din was surprised to meet Khwajah Uthman Harwani, his former mentor and guide. It was Khwajah Harwani who urged him to proceed to India and spread the message of Islam in that country. Although Muslims first entered India during the early part of the eighth century under the inspirational leadership of young Muhammad ibn al-Qasim (see chapter 20), the majority of India's population were still Hindus, which no doubt prompted Mu'in al-Din to go to India and take the message of Islam to the idolatrous Hindus. However, according to some of Mu'in al-Din's biographers, it was the Prophet Muhammad who appeared to him in the form of a dream and urged him to proceed to India to propagate Islam.

Either way, he left Ghazna and reached Lahore in 1190 CE. As a prominent centre of Islamic learning and commerce, Lahore at the time was the home of some of the subcontinent's most prominent Islamic scholars and Sufis. Here, Mu'in al-Din stayed for a period and visited the tomb of Ali al-Hujwiri (better known as Data Ganj Bakhsh) and engaged in prayers and meditation for several weeks. From Lahore, he moved to Multan and stayed there for about five years. During his stay in Multan, he learnt Sanskrit and a number of other prominent Indian languages and dialects and made preparations to move further into India. It was during his travels that he attracted a considerable following. Indeed, his asceticism and spirituality captured the imagination of people of all faiths, thus establishing his reputation as a celebrated scholar and practitioner of Islamic spirituality.

After reaching Delhi with his followers, he settled in Ajmer (in the Indian State of Rajasthan). He was now in his mid-fifties and decided to devote the rest of his life to the propagation of Islam in the subcontinent. Most of his biographers have written stories about his miracles and supernatural events. But a close study of his life proves that he was far from being a magician or a miracle worker. He was deeply engaged with the traditional Islamic sciences and *tasawwuf* (Islamic spirituality). Mu'in al-Din was a humble and kind scholar and Sufi. He was motivated by a desire to attain personal purity and teach the message of Islam in India. He was a genuine practitioner of Islamic spirituality. He did not consider himself to be special nor did he claim to possess any form of supernatural powers. However, some of his followers subsequently exaggerated his actions and achievements.

Mu'in al-Din was the founder of the *chishtiyah* Sufi Order in India but he was not the originator of the *chishtiyah* tariqa as such. That credit must go to Khwajah Ishaq Chishti, who was an outstanding champion of Sufism and a native of Chisht (in Herat in present-day Afghanistan). He inspired his leading disciples to settle in different parts of Transoxiana and Khurasan and establish *chishtiyah zawiyah* (lodges) across that region. As a result, this Sufi Order became very popular across Persia and Muslim Central Asia. However, over time, the *chishtiyah* tariqa began to lose its strength and public appeal. As with the other well-known Sufi Orders, the followers of this tariqa traced their spiritual lineage back to the Prophet through Caliph Ali ibn Abi Talib. They believed he had communicated special knowledge to the famous Hasan al-Basri (see chapter 15). Hasan then conveyed this knowledge to his Sufi successors. Thus, the originator of the *chishtiyah* Order claimed to have received special spiritual knowledge, as did many other prominent Sufis.

After settling in Ajmer, Mu'in al-Din and his disciples mixed freely with the locals and engaged them in discussion and debate on religious and spiritual matters. As a fierce critic of all forms of racial and cultural segregation, he opposed the Hindu caste system and instead argued that all human beings are equal in the sight of Allah. 'We are all children of Adam and Hawa,' he argued, 'and both Adam and Hawa were made from clay.' He led a simple, austere but active life, and never failed to emphasise the need for personal purification. Likewise, he encouraged all his disciples to regularly engage in spiritual retreats and strive to move closer to the Divine proximity. His message of love, peace, compassion, equality, freedom and brotherhood struck a chord with Muslims and Hindus alike. Thanks to his efforts, thousands of non-Muslims embraced Islam, and his disciples travelled across India to disseminate the message of Islam.

Moreover, he regularly reminded his disciples to perform the fundamental Islamic rites and rituals such as the five daily prayers, fasting during the month of Ramadan and pilgrimage to Makkah. Indeed, he was such a rigorous follower of the Prophetic *Sunnah* that he married twice in his advanced age and also urged his disciples to fulfil this important Prophetic *Sunnah*.

After more than forty years of preaching and propagating Islam in the subcontinent, Mu'in al-Din and his disciples had completely transformed the fortunes of Islam throughout that vast region. His great efforts and achievements earned him widespread approval even during his lifetime. However, after his death, he became a household name in India, Pakistan and Bangladesh. Even famous rulers, like Sultan Qutb al-Din Aybak (b. 1150-d. 1210 CE) and Sultan Shams al-Din Iltutmish (d. 1236 CE) of the Mamluk (Slave) dynasty, greatly admired him. The Mughal Emperor Akbar the Great used to travel to and from Ajmer on foot out of respect for Mu'in al-Din, the great saint of Ajmer. Likewise, Emperors Jahangir, Shah Jahan and Aurangzeb became followers of the *chishtiyah tariqa* and regularly went to Ajmer to pay homage to him.

Mu'in al-Din died in Ajmer at the ripe old age of around ninety-seven. After his death, his mission was continued by his disciples, including Hamid al-Din Sufi and Khwajah Qutb al-Din Bakhtiyar

Kaki, among others. Over time, this *tariqa* spread throughout the subcontinent, thanks to prominent *chishtiyah* Sufis like Farid al-Din Ganj-i Shakar (Baba Farid), Nizam al-Din Awliyah, Amir Khusraw and Abd al-Quddus Gangohi. Even Shaykh Ahmad Sirhindi (see chapter 81) and Shah Waliullah (see chapter 86) were heavily influenced by the religious ideas and thoughts of Khwajah Mu'in al-Din Chishti.

63

Fakhr al-Din al-Razi (b.1149 - d.1210 CE) / (b.544 - d.606 AH)

Through the support provided by Harun al-Rashid, the Abbasid Caliph (see chapter 28), and his son al-Ma'mun (see chapter 33), ancient Greek scientific, philosophical and medical works were translated into Arabic for the first time. This happened during the eighth and early part of the ninth century. At the time Baghdad, the capital of the Abbasid Caliphate, became such a prominent centre of intellectual and educational activity that students and scholars from across the Muslim world flocked to the city to study and conduct research in the Islamic sciences, philosophy, medicine, mathematics and other subjects, under the guidance of its leading scholars.

The intrusion of Greek philosophy into the Muslim world created a huge religious controversy between the Islamic traditionalists and the Neoplatonists. The traditionalists were inspired by influential Islamic scholars like Imam Ahmad ibn Hanbal (see chapter 31). They launched a severe attack on the Neoplatonic ideas of the early Muslim philosophers. This led to a clash of worldviews which has continued to continue down the centuries. After Abul Hasan al-Ash'ari's (see chapter 42) stinging critique of rationalism (Mu'tazilism) during the early part of the tenth century,

Imam al-Ghazali (see chapter 56) emerged in the eleventh century to defend, like his illustrious predecessor, the cause of Islamic traditionalism.

Al-Ghazali struck a powerful argument against the Neoplatonic theories of al-Kindi (see chapter 35), Abu Bakr al-Razi (see chapter 39), al-Farabi (see chapter 41) and Ibn Sina (see chapter 52). His critique of Neoplatonism paved the way for the emergence of Fakhr al-Din al-Razi. He became one of the most celebrated Islamic theologians of the twelfth century. Along with al-Ash'ari and al-Ghazali, he is today considered to be one of the most influential Muslim theologians of all time.

Muhammad ibn Umar, better known as Fakhr al-Din al-Razi, was born in the northern Persian city of Rayy (near modern Tehran) into a distinguished family of Islamic scholars and jurists. His father, Diya al-Din Umar, was widely respected across the city of Rayy for his vast knowledge of Islam. He was also a popular *khatib* (preacher) at his local mosque, where he regularly led Friday congregational prayers. Young al-Razi was taught by his learned father and studied Arabic, Persian, the Qur'an, and *Hadith* (Prophetic traditions) and *fiqh* (Islamic jurisprudence) at home. After completing his early education, he pursued higher education in *ilm al-kalam* (speculative theology), *falsafah* (philosophy) and aspects of natural sciences and medicine under the guidance of outstanding scholars like Simnani, al-Jili and al-Baghawi, among others.

Like his father, al-Razi was a believer in the theology of Ash'ari. He was blessed with a sharp intellect and an equally powerful memory and was a limitless seeker of knowledge and wisdom. He was keen to learn more so he left his native Rayy and moved to Maraghah (in present-day Azerbaijan) to study the philosophical sciences of the day under the guidance of Majd al-Din al-Jili. As an outstanding authority on philosophy and a teacher al-Suhrawardi (see chapter 64), al-Jili was a famous *ishraqi* philosopher and mystic. He exercised a huge influence on al-Razi's philosophical thoughts.

Al-Razi was brought up and educated at a time when Neoplatonic thought – as promoted by al-Farabi and Ibn Sina – was being scrutinised and reassessed by traditional Muslim academics. Inspired no doubt by al-Ghazali's criticism of Neoplatonic thought, al-Razi too developed a sceptical attitude towards philosophy. He became familiar with al-Ghazali's religious ideas, philosophical thoughts and intellectual worldview through al-Jili whose own teacher, had been a student of al-Ghazali. Al-Razi developed considerable doubts about Neoplatonic thought but, unlike al-Ghazali, he adopted a more moderate approach to philosophy rather than rejecting it totally.

By the time he had moved to Khwarazm, in modern Uzbekistan, he was already recognised as a master of traditional Islamic sciences, speculative theology and philosophy. He was also familiar with mathematics, medicine and the natural sciences. As it happens, his mastery of speculative theology and philosophy was such that he went to Khwarazm to challenge the ideas of the Mu'tazilite. They had become very active in that part of the world after being kicked out of Baghdad by the traditionalists. They were banished from the highest posts of the Abbasid administration by the traditionally-minded Caliph Mutawakkil 'ala Allah (b. 822-d. 861 CE).

Because of the Caliph's anti-Mu'tazilite policies,. the followers of Mu'tazilism were forced to flee from Baghdad and regroup in and around Khwarazm. Al-Razi was determined to take the fight directly to the Mu'tazilites. He was an ambitious young theologian and philosopher so he moved to that region to engage the prominent Mu'tazilite thinkers in philosophical and theological debate. Thanks to his polished debating skills and vast learning, he successfully rejected and exposed the contradictions within Mu'tazilite ideas. His Mu'tazilite opponents were unable to answer his criticism so they wanted him out of the town of Khwarazm. To this end, they started a popular revolt against al-Razi which forced him to leave the region.

From Khwarazm, he travelled to Bukhara and from there he went to Samarqand and eventually returned to his native Rayy. Soon he set out again, this time in the direction of Transoxiana, and travelled as far as the Indian territories of Punjab and Multan. His trips to India were facilitated by the Ghurid ruler, Ghiyath al-Din Muhammad and his brother, Mu'izz al-Din Muhammad. The Ghurid Kingdom in its glory days extended all the way from the shores of the Caspian Sea to the inner frontiers of India. The Ghurids were once the protectors of the Ghaznavids and the Seljuks, but later they created an independent kingdom of their own under the leadership of Ala al-Din.

The Ghurid ruler was impressed by the depth and breadth of al-Razi's learning and offered him a well-paid and high-powered gGovernmental post. This improved his personal and financial difficulties. However, intense jealousy and continuous rivalry between the gGovernment officials, coupled with rumours of political plots, soon forced him to quit his job and move to Ghazna in 1185. There he lectured on traditional Islamic sciences and philosophy for a while before finally settling in Herat. Here the local ruler constructed a religious seminary for al-Razi, and he began to teach Islamic sciences. When his name began to spread in and around Herat, students flocked from far and wide to listen to his illuminating lectures on the Qur'an, *Hadith*, *fiqh*, *kalam* and *falsafah*.

As an outspoken promoter of Islam, al-Razi never shied away from religious or philosophical controversies. Rather, he became a champion of traditional Islam and never hesitated to attack those he considered to be heretical or misguided in their approach to Islamic beliefs and practices. His criticisms were robust and sharp and, often, his opponents felt the impact of his intellectual attack. The Karramiyah, founded by Muhammad ibn Karram (d. 869 CE), were one such group. They became so angry by his stinging critique of their beliefs and practices that they attempted to assassinate him. But the determined al-Razi remained as firm as ever. Like al-Ash'ari and al-Ghazali, he was not only an outstanding intellectual, but he was also an unrelenting champion of Islamic orthodoxy. And, like his two illustrious predecessors, he possessed a powerful literary talent which he utilised better than any other scholar of his generation.

Author of more than one hundred books on all the sciences of his time, al-Razi was a truly gifted scholar and fountain of knowledge. Although he wrote prolifically on a wide range of subjects, it was his theological and philosophical contributions which made him popular across the Muslim world. His most famous theological work includes *al-Arba'in fi Usul al-Din* (Forty Questions on Religious Principles).

He was influenced by *imam al-haramayn* Abd al-Malik ibn Yusuf al-Juwayni (b. 1028-d. 1085 CE) and al-Ghazali. In his books, he provided a systematic explanation of Ash'arite theology. His *Mafatih al-Ghayb*, (The Keys to the Unseen), better known as *Tafsir al-Kabir* (The Exhaustive Commentary), is an outstanding Qur'anic commentary and a voluminous encyclopaedia of Islamic sciences. A lifelong student of the Qur'an, al-Razi thoroughly researched the *tafsir* literature before he sat down to write this monumental commentary on the Qur'an. Any learned scholar will appreciate the author's vast intellect and sheer breadth of learning after only a quick browse through this commentary.

Likewise, his major philosophical contributions include 'The Remarks and Admonitions' and 'The Sources of Wisdom'. In these books, al-Razi critically analysed and reviewed the philosophical thoughts of the Muslim Neoplatonists from the perspective of traditional Islam. Unlike al-Ghazali, he was not an opponent of philosophical sciences; rather he was only critical of certain aspects of Neoplatonic thought. His philosophical writings therefore represented a powerful mixture between *Mashsha'iyyah falsafah* (Peripatetic philosophy) and *ilm al-kalam* (speculative theology). His successful unification was a truly remarkable achievement considering that the conflict between these two intellectual traditions had been raging in the Muslim world for many centuries.

Thus, in his 'Noble Pursuits of the Science of Divinity', he developed a mixed approach to Islamic theology by combining the methods of the philosophers with the logic of the *mutakallimun* (speculative theologians). By doing this, he developed his own theological views. This also helped him to unify the thoughts of the philosophers with those of the theologians. In addition to this, al-Razi wrote prolifically on *Hadith* literature, Islamic jurisprudence, comparative religion, history, mathematics and the natural sciences. As such, his *Jami al-Ulum* (The Encyclopaedia of Sciences) was a vast compilation of traditional Islamic sciences.

Al-Razi was not only an outstanding theologian, philosopher and Islamic scholar, he was also a devout Muslim who regularly performed *nafl* (optional) prayers and observed voluntary fasts when, of course, he was not too busy reading and writing. After dedicating his entire life to the pursuit of knowledge and wisdom – and having also gained widespread recognition for his vast learning and scholarship – towards the end of his life, he completely abandoned the rationalistic methods of the philosophers and devoted all his time and energy to the study of the Qur'an.

Nevertheless, his religious thoughts had considerable influence on many renowned Muslim scholars, such as Nasir al-Din al-Tusi (see chapter 68) and his students. Indeed, his influence can even be detected in the works of such prominent modern-day Muslim scholars as Muhammad Abduh (see chapter 92), Mawlana Muhammad Akram Khan, Muhammad al-Tahir ibn Ashur, Abdullah Yusuf Ali and Leopold Weiss (Muhammad Asad). But it is his *Tafsir al-Kabir*, that famous and encyclopaedic commentary on the Qur'an, which has immortalised his name. To acquire a thorough understanding of the Qur'an and delve deeper into the multi-layered meaning of the Divine message, all serious students and scholars of Islam will continue to consult this massive commentary for a long time to come.

He was hailed as *shaykh al-Islam* (leading authority on Islam) and *sultan al-mutakallimun* (chief of the theologians). Al-Razi died at the age of fifty-nine or sixty-one and was buried in Herat, located in present-day Afghanistan.

64

Shihab al-Din Suhrawardi (b.1154 - d.1191 CE) / (b.549 - d.587 AH)

As the father of *falsafah* (Islamic philosophy), the career of al-Kindi, better known in the Latin West as Alkindus (see chapter 35), succeeded in the ninth century during the reign of Abbasid Caliphs al-Ma'mun, (see chapter 33), al-Mu'tasim Bi'llah and al-Wathiq Bi'llah. Thanks to his profound knowledge and understanding of traditional Islamic sciences and ancient Greek thought, he played a key role in the development of Islamic philosophical thought which later became known as *Mashsha'iyah* (Peripatetic) philosophy.

After al-Kindi, scores of renowned Muslim philosophers, like Abu Bakr al-Razi (see chapter 39), al-Farabi (see chapter 41) and Ibn Sina (see chapter 52), emerged in the Islamic East. They carried out a detailed study of the Islamic sources in relation to the ancient Greek philosophical heritage. They tried to reconcile between the opposing Islamic scriptural sources and Hellenistic thought.

As *Mashsha'iyah* philosophy captured the minds of the Muslim intellectuals in many parts of the Islamic East, the celebrated figure of al-Ghazali (see chapter 56) emerged in the eleventh century to launch a powerful intellectual attack on the Peripatetic thought of al-Razi, al-Farabi and Ibn Sina. Following al-Ghazali's stinging critique of Peripatetism, philosophy declined in the Islamic East. But it was later revived in the Islamic West by major Muslim philosophers like Ibn Bajjah, Ibn Tufayl (see chapter 58) and Ibn Rushd (see chapter 60). At a time when the Islamic East turned its back on Peripatetic philosophy – and the Islamic West openly embraced what the East had rejected – Shihab al-Din Suhrawardi emerged to develop a powerful blend between Peripatetic philosophy and spirituality.

Shihab al-Din Yahya ibn Habash Suhrawardi, also known as *Shaykh al-Ishraq* (Master of Illumination), was born in Suhraward in North-western Persia. He received his early education in Arabic, Persian and traditional Islamic sciences in his town. As a gifted student, he completed his primary and secondary studies while he was still in his early teens. He then developed a keen interest in philosophical sciences and spirituality. He was eager to pursue higher education in Islamic philosophical sciences. So, he left his native Suhraward and moved to Maraghah to study under the guidance of Majd al-Din al-Jili, an outstanding Persian scholar, who was teaching and researching at an educational centre there. Suhrawardi completed his advanced education in the religious sciences, philosophy and spirituality while he was still in his early twenties.

He then left Maraghah and went to the historic Persian city of Isfahan. There he conducted research in logic and philosophical sciences under the guidance of great scholars like al-Mardini and al-Farisi. They introduced him to the writings of the famous logician, al-Sawi. He travelled extensively during this period and visited Anatolia and other prominent Islamic cities, before finally settling in Aleppo. Suhrawardi lived during one of the most politically turbulent periods in Islamic history. It was when the Crusaders emerged from Europe and threatened to overwhelm the Islamic East.

After Salah al-Din had consolidated his power base in Egypt and then Syria, Iraq, Western Arabia and parts of North Africa, including Tunisia. He carved out a vast empire from Yemen to Tunisia and successfully united the Islamic East under his able leadership and defeated the European Crusaders and recaptured *al-Quds* (Jerusalem). Suhrawardi may have been motivated to move to Aleppo in the hope of attracting the attention of the Ayyubid rulers who were known for their support for learning and artistic pursuits.

As a multitalented young intellectual, it did not take long for him to establish his reputation in Aleppo as an intelligent scholar.

However, according to some historians, it was the governor of Aleppo, Malik al-Zahir Ghazi, Sultan Salah al-Din's youngest son, who summoned Suhrawardi to his court and offered him a highly paid government post. Either way, as soon as they met, they became good friends and regularly engaged in intellectual discussion on all aspects of religious sciences, philosophy and spirituality. Young Malik al-Zahir Ghazi was so impressed with Suhrawardi's learning that he began to study philosophy and Islamic mysticism under his guidance.

Although he became a great writer in both Arabic and Persian while he was still in his early twenties, Suhrawardi authored most of his influential books in Arabic after he arrived in Aleppo in 1183 CE. These included *Hikmat al-Ishraq* (The Philosophy of Illumination). He began work on this, which is his most influential philosophical work, during his journey in Anatolia and Syria while he was in his late twenties and completed it in Aleppo. In addition to this, he composed scores of other booklets on both beliefs and *batini* (inner) matters, including 'The Luminous Bodies' and *Bustan al-Qulub* (The Garden of the Hearts).

However, his philosophical works had a huge influence on Muslim philosophers and mystics, especially in Persia. Like Ibn Sina, he analysed Peripatetic philosophy in a new way, but he did not agree with everything thate Ibn Sina former wrote. Indeed, he rejected some of Ibn Sina's philosophical ideas and refined others. Having thoroughly absorbed the philosophical and spiritual thoughts of the early Muslim thinkers, Suhrawardi then analysed and evaluated their ideas and developed a fresh and alternative understanding of the Islamic scriptural sources in the light of his investigations.

Suhrawardi may have written commentaries on Ibn Sina's 'The Remarks and Admonitions' and portions of the Qur'an and Hadith but he was more than just a commentator. In fact, he was an original thinker who mastered Islamic sciences, Peripatetic philosophy, Sufi thought and ancient Zoroastrian wisdom, in addition to information from many other sources. By doing this, he developed a powerful blend between mystical philosophy and the Neoplatonic thought of the early Muslim philosophers. He did this even though al-Ghazali had already attacked them for compromising Islamic principles in their eagerness to harmonise Greek philosophy with the Islamic tradition.

The blend created by Suhrawardi became known as the *hikmat al-ishraq* ('philosophy of illumination'). The supporters of 'illuminationism' considered this to be a distinct and comprehensive system of thought because it went beyond the philosophical contradictions within the Peripatetic thought of Ibn Sina and others. At the same time, he reinforced the illuminationist dimension of philosophy and mysticism within the broader Islamic worldview. In other words, by harmonising *Mashsha'iyah* (Peripatetism), *hikmat al-Mashriqiyah* (Oriental philosophy) and *ilm al-kalam* (speculative theology) with *tasawwuf* (Islamic spirituality), Suhrawardi created a new philosophical and mystical synthesis which he presented in his major philosophical works, especially his Hikmat al-Ishraq (The Philosophy of Illumination).

Suhrawardi's 'philosophy of illumination' was the outcome of a long and ambitious intellectual project. He began by investigating all the major intellectual traditions which existed in the Islamic world at the time. He then identified and examined the theoretical foundation of the Islamic worldview. By doing this, he concluded that human reason (rationalism) had its limits. Thus, he argued that *al-Haqq* (Truth) cannot be discovered through rational effort alone. Similarly, he felt the mystical approach was not in itself sufficient for attaining the Truth – and the whole Truth. Instead, he proposed a new method which combined elements of rationality, experiential wisdom and intellectual insight. He argued that this method was more likely to lead to a deeper and more comprehensive understanding of the Truth.

By adopting a multi-disciplinary approach to Islamic thought, Suhrawardi brought the different strands of thought which existed within the Islamic world at the time under one philosophical banner, namely the 'philosophy of illumination'. This way, he demonstrated that the conflict between Neoplatonism, *ilm al-kalam* (speculative theology), *tasawwuf* (spirituality) and ancient Persian wisdom was not as deep-rooted as previously thought. He also pointed out that the core elements of these traditions had much in common. Thus, they were, in his opinion, far from being outside the intellectual tradition of Islam.

Suhrawardi was heavily influenced by the philosophical thought of Ibn Sina and became a committed Neoplatonist during his early years. But, after reportedly seeing Aristotle in a vision, he became aware of the weaknesses in Neoplatonic thought. This prompted him to find a philosophical alternative to it. After many years of intensive study and research, he finally discovered the 'philosophy of illumination'. He considered it to be a far superior system of thought than Peripatetic philosophy. However, when his new philosophical and mystical ideas became known to his opponents (especially those based at Malik al-Zahir Ghazi's court in Aleppo), they accused him of corrupting the young governor by introducing him to un-Islamic ideas and practices.

Since Sultan Salah al-Din Ayyubi and his family members were strict Sunni Muslims, the charge of promoting a non-traditional belief system (consisting of parts of Zoroastrianism, Neoplatonic thought and Shi'a theology and mysticism) was bound to offend the senior courtiers at Aleppo. As a result, Suhrawardi's opponents pressured Malik al-Zahir Ghazi to put him on trial for promoting heretical beliefs and practices. The young governor flatly refused to do so. Indeed, Malik al-Zahir Ghazi's refusal to obey the courtiers' demands prompted them to send a petition directly to Sultan Salah al-Din. This petition by a judge stated that Suhrawardi championed heretical theological and philosophical views which were similar to those of the Isma'ilis. It urged Sultan Salah al-Din to order his son to execute Suhrawardi. Sultan Salah al-Din agreed with the petition and ordered his son to put Suhrawardi to death.

In normal circumstances, the Sultan would probably have investigated this matter further before sentencing Suhrawardi to death. But at the time he was facing an imminent attack from the Crusaders and therefore decided not to upset the senior courtiers in Aleppo by refusing to comply with their demand. *Shaykh al-ishraq* (the master of the 'philosophy of illumination') was sentenced to death at the age of around thirty-seven. However, within such a short life span, he managed to author a large collection of books on a wide range of topics. In addition, he founded a new school of philosophical-cum-mystical thought which is today influential in Iran, parts of Iraq, India and Pakistan, especially within the Shi'a intellectual circles.

Not surprisingly, Suhrawardi's religious, philosophical and mystical ideas have influenced many prominent Shi'a thinkers like al-Shahrazuri (b. 1181-d. 1288 CE), Dawwani (b. 1426-d. 1502 CE), Mulla Sadra (see chapter 82) and Kumijani (d. 1895 CE).

Since his works were not translated into Western languages until relatively recently, his ideas did not gain much currency in the West although this situation is now changing, thanks to the efforts of scholars like Henry Corbin, Seyyed Hossein Nasr, John Walbridge, Hossein Ziai and Mehdi Aminrazavi.

65

Ibn al-Arabi
(b.1165 - d.1240 CE) /
(b.561 - d.638 AH)

After the establishment of Umayyad rule in Spain at the beginning of the eighth century, brilliant Umayyad rulers like Abd al-Rahman III (see chapter 43) and al-Hakam (b. 915-d. 976 CE) transformed the fortunes of *al-Andalus* (Spain). Though their rule represented one of the most glorious periods in the history of Western Islam, the Umayyads were eventually overthrown in 1031 CE. This led to the chaotic period of 'the small States' which continued for more than half a century before the North African *al-Murabitun* (al-Moravid) ruler Yusuf ibn Tashfin marched into Spain and reunited the country under his leadership. Peace and security were restored across Spain until the al-Moravids lost their grip on power in 1145 CE.

As disorder spread throughout the land, another North African power, the *al-Muwahhidun* (al-Mohads) led by Abd al-Mu'min, defeated the rebels and again restored peace across Spain. The al-Mohads ruled Spain for about a century, but disorder returned. This was a chaotic period in Islamic Spain when successive political dynasties emerged and took control of the country but failed to maintain their grip on power. During this political confusion, one of the Muslim world's most influential spiritual philosophers surfaced to develop a powerful and, equally, controversial metaphysical theory. This remarkable thinker, poet and writer was Ibn al-Arabi.

Muhyi al-Din Muhammad ibn Ali al-Arabi, known as shaykh al-akbar (the Great Master), was born in *Mursiyah* (Murcia) in Islamic Spain. He was also known as Ibn Arabi – without the definite article al – to distinguish him from the famous *qadi* (Muslim jurist) Abu Bakr ibn al-Arabi (b. 1076-d. 1148 CE). His father, Ali, was a civil servant in the government of Muhammad ibn Sa'id, who was an independent ruler of Murcia until the al-Mohad ruler Abu Yaqub Yusuf marched into Murcia, Valencia and Lorca and occupied those territories. This forced the family to move to Seville and begin to rebuild their lives. As the son of a respected civil servant and Sufi sage, Ibn al-Arabi grew up to be a sensible, intelligent and disciplined young man. During his early years, he received training in Arabic language, literature and aspects of the traditional Islamic sciences.

As he was fascinated by *ilm al-tasawwuf* (Sufism or Islamic spirituality), he studied and acquired deeper insights into Islamic spirituality while he was still in his teens. According to Ibn al-Arabi, he was fifteen when he met Ibn Rushd (Averroes – see chapter 60), the famous Muslim of Spain. Ibn Rushd was impressed by his grasp of Islamic teachings and spirituality. After marrying at a young age, he worked as a secretary to the governor of Seville. During the next decade, Ibn al-Arabi received an advanced education in Islamic sciences, including *tafsir* (Qur'anic commentary), *Hadith* (Prophetic traditions) and *fiqh* (Islamic jurisprudence). He specialised in *zahiri* (literal) legal thought (as championed by Ibn Hazm al-Andalusi – see chapter 53) and studied under the guidance of some of Seville and Ceuta's leading Islamic scholars.

Then, at the age of thirty, he left Spain and moved to North Africa. His stay in Tunis must have awakened his desire to explore the eastern heartlands of Islam. Although he claimed to have been instructed in the form of a vision to go to the East. Either way, in the year 1200 CE, he journeyed to the Islamic East where he remained for the rest of his life. Two years later, Ibn al-Arabi went to Makkah to perform the sacred *hajj* and, during his stay there, he made friends with a Persian mystic whose pious and attractive daughter inspired him to compose his, 'The Interpreter of Desires', which is a small but elegant collection of spiritual and romantic poems.

For the next two decades, he travelled extensively in search of knowledge and received advanced training in all aspects of Islamic spirituality. After visiting Baghdad, Makkah, Madinah, Aleppo, Mosul, parts of Central Asia and Turkey, he eventually settled in Damascus in 1223 CE with his small group of disciples. By then, he was an absolute master of traditional Islamic sciences including *tafsir*, *Hadith*, *fiqh* and *ilm al-kalam* (speculative theology) and was recognised as a specialist in Sufism. Like many other Muslim scholars of the past, he acquired such a mastery of Islamic sciences that his close disciples considered him to be an exceptionally gifted practitioner of Islamic principles and practices.

However, what set Ibn al-Arabi apart from his peers were his inner qualities, spiritual attainments and powerful imagination. In other words, his profound knowledge and understanding of Islamic spirituality combined with his extraordinary ability to communicate his spiritual teachings to his disciples, both verbally and in writing, established him as one of the Muslim world's most gifted metaphysicians and prolific writers. Metaphysics is the branch of philosophy that studies the basic nature of reality. He was a master of traditional Islamic sciences and was keen to distinguish the *zahiri* ('outer') reality of Islamic rituals from the *batini* ('inner') features of Islamic principles, teachings and practices.

The 'men of reason', according to Ibn al-Arabi, focus all their attention on the 'form' and external features of religious practices while the 'men of vision' seek to rise above the 'form' to reach the 'substance' and soul of religious experience. Thus, the formal religious teachers (like the theologians and jurists) practice and observe the 'outer' dimension of religion, but the Sufis (or mystics) long for the *kashf* ('unveiling') of the *al-Haqq* (Ultimate Reality) before the eye of the heart to attain spiritual light. Ibn al-Arabi claimed to have attained spiritual 'unveiling' relatively easily. During one of his spiritual retreats, he claimed, he was blessed with a series of mystical inspirations and insights which he recorded in the form of books, manuscripts and letters.

He and his disciples believed this to be an inner *nur* (light) granted to him by Allah. He also claimed to have been blessed with numerous supernatural experiences and visions (including encounters with the Prophet Muhammad, Jesus and some of his spiritual masters). Although he was a strict follower of Islam in its *zahiri* (outer) form, Ibn al-Arabi nevertheless felt he needed to dive deep into the ocean of *tasawwuf* (the inner spirituality of Islam) to explore its limits and possibilities, even if it meant it upset the religious orthodoxy.

In addition to the Qur'an and Hadith, he surveyed Platonic, Neoplatonic, Hermetic, Gnostic and Isma'ili literature. He absorbed their outer ideas, before developing his own metaphysical theory. Ibn al-Arabi possessed a powerful mind which enabled him to draw information from many different and conflicting sources. In doing so, he developed a comprehensive metaphysical system which continues to influence Islamic spiritual thinkers to this day. Unlike Abd al-Qadir al-Jilani (see chapter 57), Mu'in al-Din Chishti (see chapter 62), Jalal al-Din Rumi (see chapter 69) and Baha al-Din Naqshband (see chapter 74), he did not start a Sufi *tariqa* (Order) nor a *madhhab* (school of thought). Instead, he devoted all his time and intellectual energy to communicating his spiritual thoughts in books for future generations.

Apart from a few close disciples whom he taught and initiated into his mystical ways, he was not in the habit of surrounding himself with a large crowd of followers, unlike the other great Sufi masters of the past. Indeed, his main objective was to formulate a complete mystical philosophy so that the scholars, Sufi masters as well as the public could draw on it as and when they needed to satisfy their intellectual and spiritual needs.

To achieve this objective, he wrote at a phenomenal rate. As a mystical thinker and one of the Muslim world's most prolific writers, he provided a supernatural explanation for his astonishing literary output. According to Ibn al-Arabi, as soon as he engaged in a spiritual retreat, mystical thoughts flooded into his mind like a storm. Thus, writing was an effortless process for him. According to some of his biographers, he authored as many as eight hundred books on all aspects of Islamic mystical thought. Others claim he wrote no more than a few hundred books. However, all his biographers agree that many of his works have remained in manuscript form, still waiting to be edited and published for the first time. Of his published works, the most famous are *Al-Futuhat al-Makkiyyah* (The Makkan Revelations), which as the title suggests, was written during his stay in Makkah and the *Fusus al-Hikam* (The Bezels of Wisdom) was written in Damascus.

The *Futuhat* consists of more than five hundred chapters. It is an encyclopaedia of religious and spiritual sciences. In this book, Ibn al-Arabi provided a comprehensive mystical interpretation of fundamental Islamic religious practices, including *salat*, *siyam*, *hajj* and *zakat*. He also explained the nature of the various mystical stages which the Sufis pass through during their spiritual journey. Through this process, he developed a spiritual interpretation of various Qur'anic verses and Prophetic traditions. Moreover, he explored the meaning of *al-Asma wa'l Sifat* (the ninety-nine Divine Names and Attributes) as mentioned in the Qur'an and Prophetic traditions.

Ibn al-Arabi may have been a prolific writer, but he was far from being an organised thinker. The mystical thoughts he communicated in his *Futuhat* are not presented logically or clearly; rather he wrote as and when ideas appeared to him and did so without giving much thought to their context or format. However, the same cannot be said about his *Fusus al-Hikam*, which is probably his most popular book. In it he claimed to have presented a systematic interpretation of Islamic mystical philosophy as revealed to twenty-seven Prophets, beginning with Adam and concluding with Muhammad, the *Khatm al-Anbiya* (the Seal of the Prophets). The popularity of this book is most evident from the fact that more than one hundred commentaries have been written on it.

In these and other books, Ibn al-Arabi developed a mystical philosophy which was influential and controversial. Indeed, his metaphysical theory was based on the view that at a certain level, all Being is fundamentally One (this is called *Wahdat al-Wujud*). At another level, everything is only a manifestation of the Divine. Although metaphysically speaking, he made a fine distinction between Allah's *wujud* and that of His creatures (in the sense that Allah's *wujud* was *wajib* (a necessity) and His creatures were *mumkin* (dependent). His critics argued that his distinction between the two was not sufficiently clear. That is why they accused him of promoting pantheistic beliefs. However, according to Ibn al-Arabi's disciples, such misunderstandings arose because his critics took passages from his *Futuhat* out of context, and they failed to understand his metaphysical theory in its entirety.

In fact, Ibn al-Arabi's concept of *Wahdat al-Wujud* (Oneness of Being), his mystical interpretation of *al-Asma wa'l Sifat* (Divine

Names and Attributes), his notion of *al-Insan al-Kamil* (Perfect Man) and his claim to have been the Seal of Muhammadan Sanctity proved hugely controversial. Thus, some of his most severe critics such as Ibn Taymiyyah (see chapter 72), Shaykh Ahmad Sirhindi (see chapter 81) and others accused him of misinterpreting traditional Islamic sources. They also criticised him for 'twisting' the meaning of *Tawhid* (Divine oneness) and for deifying the Prophet. They also accused him of making all religions equal, and of idolising women, among many other things.

However, his views were strongly defended by other equally distinguished Islamic scholars like al-Firuzabadi (b. 1329-d. 1414 CE), Jalal al-Suyuti (b. 1445-d. 1505 CE) and Shah Waliullah (see chapter 86). To be fair to Ibn al-Arabi, even his harshest critics raised objections only against certain aspects of his thought. They did not consider his entire metaphysical theory to be heretical or unacceptable as such. Even Ibn Taymiyyah, who along with Shaykh Ahmad Sirhindi was one of Ibn al-Arabi's most fierce critics, accepted this fact (Ibn Taymiyyah himself was linked to the Sufi tradition of Abd al-Qadir al-Jilani). As for Shaykh Ahmad Sirhindi, he proposed *wahdat* al-*shuhud* (Oneness of Being in perception, or unity of witnesses) to correct Ibn al-Arabi's *Wahdat al-Wujud* (Oneness of Being). Nevertheless, Ibn al-Arabi's mystical philosophy has indeed been hugely influential in the Muslim world.

This is most evident from the fact that leading Islamic scholars, reformers and spiritual guides like Mulla Sadra (see chapter 82), Shah Waliullah, Shaykh Ahmad Sirhindi and even Sultan Muhammad (Fatih) II (see chapter 77) were influenced by Ibn al-Arabi's mystical philosophy and thought. Likewise, the religious ideas of many modern Muslim scholars and spiritual mentors, such as Rene Guenon (Abd al-Wahid Yahya), Frithjof Schuon (Isa Nur al-Din), Martin Lings (Abu Bakr Siraj al-Din), Seyyed Hossein Nasr and Charles (Hasan) Le Gai Eaton have been heavily influenced by Ibn al-Arabi's writings.

Indeed, according to Miguel Asin Palacios, an outstanding Spanish writer and an expert on Ibn al-Arabi, famous Western thinkers like Alighieri and Ramon Llull were also inspired by the *shaykh al-akbar*. Ibn al-Arabi died at the age of seventy-five and was buried in Damascus. Later, in the sixteenth century, a mausoleum was built there in his memory by the Ottoman Sultan Salim (Selim) I and it stands to this day.

66

Fatimah bint Muhammad al-Samarqandiyyah (b. n.d - d.1185 CE) / (b. n.d. - d.581 AH)

Muslim women have been torchbearers and pioneers in educational, cultural and religious scholarship. One name that stands out among these great people is Fatimah al-Samarqandiyyah. She was extraordinary and had a flawless character. She possessed a wealth of knowledge and left a huge legacy with countless contributions to Islamic history.

Fatimah al-Samarqandiyyah was the daughter of a great scholar of Islam. His name was Muhammad ibn Ahmad al-Samarqandi. He was a prominent jurist and author of *Tuhfat al-Fuqaha* (A Gift for Jurists). This is a very famous book in the *Hanafi* school of thought. Fatimah learnt from her father and had memorised this book. He passed away in 1144 CE and was known for his righteousness and for devoting his entire life to seeking and conveying knowledge to his students and family.

Fatimah's exact date of birth is unknown, but it is recorded that she was born in the 12th century in Samarqand, the third-largest city in present-day Uzbekistan and one of the oldest inhabited cities in Central Asia. Samarqand has always prospered as it was an important city on the Silk Road. Moreover, it is famous for being the home of Islamic scholars and as a fountain of Islamic sciences, arts and culture. When Fatimah was born, the city was under the control of the Mongols and the public was largely oppressed. The city had not yet reached its fame and greatness. She was not from the time of the Prophet, nor did she see the *Sahabah*, but under her father's guidance, Fatimah blossomed into a brilliant scholar of unparalleled depth and wisdom. She became one of the top *Hanafi* jurists.

Her education went beyond the limits of ritualistic worship and included the complexities of *sawm*, *zakat*, *umrah* and *hajj*, business transactions, inheritance laws, marriage and the principles of enjoining good and preventing evil. Fatimah directly learned from her father, who was her greatest teacher and mentor. She became a specialist in calligraphy, Islamic jurisprudence, Quranic sciences and Hadith to the extent that she was granted authority to issue rulings on various matters. Her fatwa (rulings) were written in her handwriting and also included her father's signature.

She was a very righteous and beautiful woman. When Fatimah reached a marriageable age, it was reported that a group of people from the lands of Byzantium came and requested her hand, as she was one of the most beautiful women of her time. Her father rejected their proposal. She may well have received other proposals from rich princes and powerful men who could have offered her the luxuries of the world. However, her father had a different and better vision for her. He intended to marry her to a pious and knowledgeable scholar. There is a fascinating story of how her marriage took place.

Abu Bakr al-Kasani was a brilliant student. He came to study by Fatimah's father and excelled in both the principles and details of Islamic jurisprudence. He then authored the book *Bada'i' al-Sana'i'* (Marvellous Artistry in the Arrangement of the Legal Regulations). This was an extensive commentary on *Tuhfat al-Fuqaha* written by Fatimah's father. The commentary was an eight-volume work that later became a classic legal text among scholars. After completing the commentary, Al-Kasani presented it to his teacher who was extremely impressed with his high scholarship. The father then decided to marry his daughter to his brilliant and pious student. The union was a unique one because Imam al-Kasani's book became the *mahr* (marriage gift) for her marriage with him. This book continues to be a major reference source for *Hanafi* school of thought across the world. This incident produced a humorous anecdote of that period: al-Kasani explained his book (A Gift for Jurists) and in return, his teacher gave him his daughter in marriage.

After the marriage, the scholarly couple lived in the same house as Fatimah's father, which resulted in the formation of an informal *fiqh* committee that would find solutions to the problems related to jurisprudence. Despite his considerable knowledge, al-Kasani often turned to Fatimah when he faced complex *fiqh* questions. Her wisdom and guidance became invaluable. She would put her signature alongside her critical comments – a testament to her exceptional grasp of Islamic jurisprudence.

History records that she was a scholar, virtuous and learned in *Hadith* who possessed beautiful handwriting. She studied under the guidance of many scholars and in turn many studied by her and when she taught. She authored many books on jurisprudence (*fiqh*) and *Hadith*.

Ibn Adim, the biographer of Aleppo, reported that his father mentioned that Fatimah was proficient in transmitting matters of her school of thought with notable precision. Her husband Imam al-Kasani would sometimes err in his legal views. Fatimah would guide him to the correct position and explain to him the reasons for his error. As a result, he would change hiser viewpoint. He also said that she used to issue fatwas (legal rulings). Her husband respected and honoured her.

The students of Fatimah's husband narrated that whenever her husband would receive a difficult *fiqh* question, he would go home with their permission and get back with a detailed answer to the question. This happened often, so they understood that al-Kasani was going home to consult with Fatimah al-Samarqandiyyah whenever he could not solve a certain issue alone. This shows the humility of her husband as he made his enquiries known to his students.

One of her lesser-known qualities was her calligraphic skills. Her beautiful and intricate writing was admirable. Fatimah created pieces of art that were highly respected and reliable. Her fatwas became works of art in themselves. In the beginning, whenever a fatwa was issued from their household, it was jointly signed by the father and daughter. Later, after she married Imam al-Kasani, the rulings were issued with three signatures by including the son-in-law, indicating a collaborative service.

Fatimah's influence extended far beyond her home. She and her husband made a courageous decision to move to Syria, a land brimming with historical knowledge. It was a journey of sacrifice, both in physical and mental terms. Leaving behind the comforts of her home and establishing a life in a new place mirrored her internal journey towards a greater aim of gaining knowledge. In Aleppo, they taught in the Umayyad Mosque. She was shown great courtesy there. Her wisdom and scholarship attracted the attention of the notable figures of her time, including Sultan Nur al-Din Zangi (see chapter 59). Fatimah became his trusted advisor and personal counsellor in complex matters of religion, *fiqh* and internal affairs of the state.

Inevitably, as an excellent scholar with great respect, she played an important role in guiding, admonishing and counselling people. Thus, she had an impact on the social affairs of her community. It is said that Nur al-Din treated her with honour. Fatimah wanted to return to Samarqand after her father's death. But the Sultan pleaded with her to stay, which she did. This indicates the significance that the Sultan had for her in his territory.

Fatimah's piety and compassion were equally remarkable. She was not just a jurist and scholar but also an exceptionally charitable person who put the needs of others before hers. Daud ibn Ali, one of the jurists of the Halawiyyah school in Aleppo, mentioned that she established the tradition of providing iftar during Ramadan for the jurists. She held two fine bracelets. She took them out and sold them. She then spent the money on preparing iftar each night. This act inspired future generations, and the practice continues to take place in Syria after all these years.

Fatimah al-Samarqandiyyah's journey through life was one of total dedication to both knowledge and piety. She passed away in Aleppo in about 1185 CE, leaving behind a legacy that continues to inspire and benefit Islamic scholarship. Her husband lived after her for about six years. Her body is buried in Masjid Ibrahim-Khalil, Aleppo. After she passed away, Imam al-Kasani visited her grave every Friday. Before his death, he succeeded in his request to be buried beside her grave.

Fatimah's story is a testament to the power of women in Islam, a reminder that their contributions to knowledge and faith have shaped the course of history and continue to guide us today. She dedicated herself to the lifelong pursuit of righteous knowledge and illuminated the path of many others on the way. Her legacy continues and is nearing one-thousand years.

67

Abul Hasan al-Shadili (b.1196 - d.1258 CE) / (b.594 - d.656 AH)

According to a famous *Hadith* (prophetic tradition), at the turn of every century, there will emerge a *mujaddid* (or religious regenerator) who will call the Muslims back to the original, pure message of Islam. Some renowned Muslim rulers, reformers and personalities like Umar ibn Abd al-Aziz (see chapter 19), Abu Hanifah (see chapter 21), Malik ibn Anas (see chapter 24), al-Shafi'i (see chapter 30), Ahmad ibn Hanbal (see chapter 31), al-Ghazali (see chapter 56), Ibn Taymiyyah (see chapter 72), Shaykh Ahmad Sirhindi (see chapter 81) and Shah Waliullah (see chapter 86) were considered to be religious regenerators of their time.

But outstanding Sufi sages like Hasan al-Basri (see chapter 15), Abd al-Qadir al-Jilani (see chapter 57), Jalal al-Din Rumi (see chapter 69), Khwajah Naqshband (see chapter 74), Shihab al-Din Abu Hafs Umar al-Suhrawardi (b. 1145-d. 1234 CE), Mu'in al-Din Chishti (see chapter 62) and Najm al-Din Kubra (b. 1145-d. 1221 CE), who contributed immensely to the protection and spreading of Islam as a religion and a way of life, were not considered to be *mujaddid* as readily as the former. Yet had it not been for the heroic efforts of these great spiritual figures of Islam, the forces of materialism and hedonism would have overwhelmed the Muslim world a long time ago.

Of the numerous Sufi *tariqa* (Orders) which emerged in the Muslim world over the last fourteen centuries, the *qadiriyah*, *naqshbandiyah* and the *chishtiyah* are the most popular and prominent. However, the Sufi Order founded by Abul Hasan al-Shadhili, the great North African Sufi scholar and sage, also played a vital role in the preservation of Islamic thought and practices in North Africa, as well as in the spreading of Islam across Europe and America.

Ali ibn Abdullah ibn Abd al-Jabbar al-Shadhili is known as Imam Shadhili. He was born in the district of Ghumara, near modern Ceuta in Morocco. His family members were devout Muslims and followers of *Maliki fiqh* (jurisprudence) and traced their lineage back to the Prophet through his grandson, Hasan ibn Ali. He was brought up and educated in an Islamic environment. Young Shadhili absorbed Islamic knowledge and wisdom from his family members before he went for further and higher education under the guidance of great teachers.

Shadhili lived during the relatively peaceful rule of the al-Mohads (this dynasty was founded by Muhammad ibn Tumart (b. 1077-d. 1130 CE), a prominent North African Islamic reformer of the time). He became a devout student of Islam from an early age. Shadhili was such a talented student that he gained recognition throughout his locality for his vast knowledge of Islamic sciences while he was still in his early twenties.

His knowledge of Islamic jurisprudence, especially *Maliki* legal thought, was so remarkable that he regularly participated in legal discussions and debates with other famous local scholars. Despite being a bright student and a skilled debater, he became bored with dry legalistic debate and argumentation. He longed for personal satisfaction and inner peace. Thus began his search for a spiritual teacher who could guide him in the ways of *tasawwuf* (Islamic spirituality) and *ma'rifa* (gnosis).

His quest for a genuine spiritual guide eventually brought him into contact with the renowned Moroccan Sufi Shaykh Abd al-Salam ibn Mashish of Fez. At the time he was based at his *zawiyah* (Sufi lodge) in Jabal al-Alam where he was engaged in spiritual retreats with his small group of disciples. When Shadhili approached Shaykh Mashish, the latter reportedly told him to go away and return after performing a full bath. When he returned after the ritual cleansing, he was told to go back and purify himself again. Shadhili did as he was told and returned once more. For the third time, Shaykh Mashish told him to go away and purify himself thoroughly.

This time Shadhili understood what the master was hinting at. Thus, he told him that he had indeed thoroughly cleansed himself of his previous habits and practices. The first cleansing act referred to the physical purification of the body. The second represented the rejection of all forms of objectionable deeds and actions. The third referred to the cleansing of the heart, mind and soul. After going through this cleansing process, the master invited Shadhili into his company and trained him in the methods of Islamic mysticism. His time with Shaykh Mashish represented a major turning point in Shadhili's life. It was during this period that he mastered the rigorous methods of Sufism and began to experience Islamic spirituality in its highest form. As the first part of his life (namely that of a *zahiri* (external) scholar who kept himself occupied with scholarly discussions and legal argumentation) came to an end, a new and fresh chapter began. This was where the pursuit of spiritual illumination, inner peace and contentment became his main priority in life.

After completing his training with Shaykh Mashish, Shadhili left his native Morocco for Shadhila in Tunisia. That is why he became known as Imam Shadhili. In Tunisia, he engaged in spiritual retreats for long periods and gathered around him a small group of followers who helped him to establish a *zawiyah* in 1228 CE. It was during one of his retreats here that he claimed to have been blessed with a vision wherein he was instructed to go out and call the locals back to the original, pure message of Islam. In response, he trained his disciples in Islamic sciences and spirituality and then sent them to the local villages to propagate Islam. This movement later became known as *tariqa al-shadhiliyah* (the *shadhiliyah* Sufi Order).

The locals responded with much enthusiasm and became followers of the *shadhiliyah* Order. Islamic spirituality – as championed by Shadhili – thus spread across Tunisia, Morocco and many other parts of North Africa during his lifetime. Indeed, the message of this tariqa became so popular that even the local ruler and his family became staunch followers of this Sufi brotherhood. Later, during his visit to the Islamic East to perform the sacred pilgrimage to Makkah, Shadhili met the Ayyubid ruler, al-Malik al-Aziz Uthman, the second son of the famous Salah al-Din Ayyubi (Saladin). He was impressed by Shadhili's spiritual accomplishments and offered him a great tower overlooking the historic Egyptian city of Alexandria to establish a *zawiyah* there. He accepted the Sultan's gift and returned to Tunisia intending to revisit Egypt later.

At the age of forty-seven, Shadhili claimed to have been blessed with another vision. In this vision, he was instructed to leave Tunisia and go to Egypt to propagate Islam there. He left North Africa and moved to Alexandria accompanied by his family, friends and disciples. Once there he he established a *shadhiliyah zawiyah* inside the multi-floored tower, given to him by the Ayyubid Sultan many years earlier. Another possible explanation for his move from Tunisia to Egypt could be that the *shadhiliyah* Order had by then become a permanent part of the North African region, and he decided to proceed to Egypt to extend its influence and establish a permanent base there.

Either way, on his arrival in Egypt, Shadhili received a warm welcome from the Egyptian people in general and the religious scholars, government officials and other Sufi groups in particular. Thus, great scholars and Sufi sages like al-Izz al-Din ibn Abd al-Salam, al-Mundhiri and al-Wasiti supported his efforts to restore Islamic teachings and spirituality.

Trained in both the *zahiri* (external) and *batini* (inner) dimensions of Islam, Shadhili developed a harmonious fusion between the practical and spiritual teachings of Islam, and through this, he won the hearts and minds of the Egyptian people. As an expert in traditional Islamic sciences, especially in *fiqh* (Islamic jurisprudence) and *Hadith* (Prophetic traditions), he constantly emphasised the importance of following Prophetic practices in the pursuit of spiritual illumination. Adherence to the Prophetic *Sunnah*, he argued, was essential for success on the spiritual path. In this respect, his understanding and interpretation of Sufism was no different from that of other great Sufis like Abd al-Qadir al-Jilani, Khwajah Naqshband and Mu'in al-Din Chishti.

To prove that there was no contradiction between the *minhaj al-Sunnah* (Prophetic way) and the ways of *tasawwuf*, he took part in the Battle of al-Mansurah (1250 CE), where the Muslims fought against the Crusaders led by St. Louis XI of France. He insisted on taking part in the battle, despite being blind, and thereby proved that one does not have to become a hermit to be a Sufi. On the contrary, he argued, it was possible to lead a normal, ordinary life, as did the Prophet Muhammad, and yet attain the peak of Islamic spirituality.

The age of Shadhili was indeed one of the most significant periods in the history of Sufism. It was during this period that scores of influential Sufis emerged in different parts of the Muslim world. They kept the flame of Islam burning across the Islamic world. They did so in the face of overwhelming political, social and cultural challenges which confronted the Muslims at the time. Some of these great luminaries included Mu'in al-Din Chishti, al-Suhrawardi and Rumi in the East, and Abu Madyan al-Andalusi, ibn al-Arabi, Mashish and Ibn Sabin in the Islamic West. These influential Sufis inspired the Muslim public to reject the forces of materialism and self-indulgence which threatened to overwhelm Islamic societies both in the East and the West.

At the same time, the Muslim world faced a serious political and military threat from the Mongol army. As it happened, the Mongols soon overran the shaky defence put up by the Muslims and marched into Baghdad in 1258 CE and reduced the great city to rubble. Shadhili received the news of the fall of Baghdad while he was on his way to Makkah to perform his last pilgrimage. As a proud Muslim, he must have been shocked and horrified by this tragedy. But, deep down, he probably knew that it was the Muslims who had brought this disaster on themselves by creating unnecessary political disunity and division within the *ummah* by championing tribal factionalism and materialistic values and practices at the expense of Islamic unity and solidarity.

Unlike, for example, Jalal al-Din Rumi or Ibn al-Arabi, Shadhili did not write any books. Instead, he preferred to explain the message of Islam and Islamic spirituality through regular lectures, which he delivered from the mosque he founded in Egypt. He also trained hundreds of disciples who spread throughout North Africa and Egypt and began to popularise his teachings. The main focus of his teachings was the attainment of inner purification and spiritual illumination through the continuous practice of *dhikr*, or declaration of Divine Names and Attributes (*al-asma wa'l sifat*). Shadhili practised and preached a balanced and moderate form of asceticism which sought to uplift and elevate the spirit, without harming the flesh.

After Shadhili's death at the age of around sixty-one, collections of his invocations, or *adkhar* (litanies), were published by his prominent disciples and later became the foundation of *shadhiliyah* teachings. These collections included 'Invocation of the Sea', Hizb al-Nasr (Invocation of Help) and 'Invocation of the Earth'. Later, the teachings of this Sufi Order flourished across North Africa (especially in Morocco) under the guidance of eminent North African Sufis like Shaykh al-Juzuli, Shaykh al-Ghazwani and al-Darqawi. Thanks to the efforts of Shaykh Illish, Shaykh al-Alawi (d. 1934 CE) and Shaykh al-Hashimi (d. 1961 CE), the teachings of this Sufi Order have also spread across Europe and America.

Distinguished European Sufis like Rene Guenon (Abd al-Wahid Yahya), Frithjof Schuon (Isa Nur al-Din Ahmad), Titus Burckhardt (Ibrahim Izz al-Din) and Martin Lings (Abu Bakr Siraj al-Din) were deeply influenced by *shadhiliyah* teachings and practices. Buried in the village of Humaithra on the coast of the Red Sea, Imam Shadhili's lasting message of Islamic morality, ethics and spirituality continues to influence millions of Muslims across North Africa, Egypt, Sudan, Turkey, Iran, parts of East Africa and the Balkans to this day.

68

Nasir al-Din al-Tusi (b.1201 - d.1274 CE) / (b.598 - d.673 AH)

The thirteenth century was one of the most destructive periods in Islamic history. As Abbasid political authority rapidly deteriorated, countless territories expanded across the Muslim world, dealing a lasting blow to Islamic political unity and solidarity. The Abbasid Caliph was increasingly seen as a mere figurehead without any real political or military power. This apparent weakness made the Islamic East vulnerable to foreign attack. In fact, the weakness of the Caliph's position became all too clear when the Mongol groups emerged from Asia and threatened to overpower the heartlands of Islam. Once a great seat of Islamic political, military and intellectual dominance, Baghdad city now was a shadow of its former self.

Thanks to the *Bait al-Hikmah* (House of Wisdom) of the early Abbasid era and the Nizamiyah College of the Seljuk period, the Muslim world once led the world in intellectual and literary activities. But following the rapid decline of Islamic political power and military might during the thirteenth century, the glorious era of Islamic political, cultural and intellectual dominance seemed to be coming to an end. During this sad and turbulent period in Islamic history, Nasir al-Din al-Tusi emerged to revive the Islamic intellectual world by founding one of Islamic history's most outstanding institutions of higher education.

Muhammad Nasir al-Din al-Tusi was born in Tus, in the Persian province of Khurasan. He was a contemporary of St. Thomas Aquinas (b. 1225-d. 1274 CE), the renowned Catholic theologian, and Albertus Magnus (b. 1200-d. 1280 CE), also known as Albert the Great. They were two of the most influential figures of European scholastic thought. Al-Tusi's father was a prominent religious scholar and jurist who ensured his son received a thorough education in Arabic, Persian and traditional Islamic sciences. He was raised in a family where learning and education were considered to be a way of life. Al-Tusi developed his thirst for knowledge and wisdom from an early age so the search for knowledge became his main occupation in life.

After completing his elementary education at home, he went to Nishapur to pursue advanced education in Islamic, philosophical and other sciences of the day. It was a thriving centre of intellectual and commercial activity and the home of the famous Nizamiyah College where the influential Abu Hamid al-Ghazali (see chapter 56) once lived and taught. Nishapur at the time attracted students from far and wide. Here he studied philosophy, mathematics and medicine under the guidance of prominent scholars like 'al-Damad', a philosopher linked to the Peripatetic school of Ibn Sina; Kamal al-Din, an eminent scientist and mathematician and Qutb al-Din al-Misri, a student of Fakhr al-Din al-Razi (see chapter 63) and also an expert authority on medical sciences.

Al-Tusi was known to have been a gifted student. He not only learned philosophy, mathematics, astronomy and other scientific subjects of his day but also mastered the traditional Islamic sciences and received *ijaza* (certification: the equivalent of a modern university degree) in *Hadith* (Prophetic traditions) when he was barely twenty-one. Although he was a Shi'a scholar of the *ithna 'ashari* (Twelver) tradition, he was admired by both the Shi'a and Sunni populations of Nishapur on account of his vast learning. He was only in his early twenties when Khurasan was invaded by the Mongols. This forced him to seek sanctuary with the followers of the neo-Isma'ili *nizari* (assassin) sect.

This extremist religious sect was founded by Hasan-i-Sabbah (b. 1050-d. 1124 CE) and became notorious for assassinating their opponents. The followers of this group were surrounded by the rough steppes of Central Asia so they created a safe haven for themselves in Alamut. It was under the sponsorship of the *nizari* leader Nasir al-Din Abd al-Rahman that al-Tusi authored many books on philosophy, logic, ethics and mathematics. His highly praised *Kitab al-Akhlaq-i-Nasiri* (The Book of Nasirean Ethics) was composed during this period. As the title indicates, it was dedicated to his patron, Nasir al-Din Abd al-Rahman.

Following the Mongol capture of Alamut in 1255 CE, al-Tusi experienced considerable personal hardship and suffering. But, impressed by his vast learning, the Mongol ruler Hulagu Khan (b. 1218-d. 1265 CE) appointed him his personal advisor. Al-Tusi was with the Mongol warlord when he launched his devastating attack on Baghdad, the seat of the Abbasid Caliphate, in 1258 CE. The destruction of Baghdad, coupled with how the reigning Abbasid Caliph al-Musta'sim (b. 1213-d. 1258 CE) was murdered, truly shocked and horrified the Muslim world. As Hulagu's advisor, he may have played some part in the massacre of Baghdad, although it is not clear how significant that role was. According to some Shi'a sources, it was al-Tusi who urged the Mongols to attack Baghdad because he was eager to bring down the Sunni Abbasid Caliphate.

But, according to other historians, this story has little credibility because Hulagu, in their opinion, would have attacked Baghdad come what might. Therefore al-Tusi could not have initiated or prevented the attack on Baghdad because he was himself entirely reliant on the goodwill of the Mongol ruler. Being no more than a useful guide and advisor to Hulagu, his position within the Mongol political hierarchy was thus a limited one.

However, the Mongol sack of Baghdad was a truly unmatched event. From being once the home of some of the Muslim world's finest schools, colleges, libraries and hospitals, the Mongols turned Baghdad into rubble. As an outstanding intellectual and writer, such mindless killing and meaningless destruction must have shocked and horrified al-Tusi, who reportedly tried to prevent the destruction of the city's libraries and hospitals but failed. His failure to save the city's libraries probably inspired al-Tusi to construct the Maraghah Observatory which later became one of the Islamic world's finest institutions of higher education and learning.

Ironically, this was achieved thanks largely to the generous support of Hulagu himself. After the Observatory was completed in 1261 CE, al-Tusi went out of his way to recruit some of the leading Muslim scholars and scientists of the day to this institution. They included al-Shirazi and al-Urdi who taught and conducted research there. Also, this institution housed more than forty thousand books on all the sciences of the day. Some of the books were most probably rescued from the ransacked libraries of Baghdad and Damascus.

As the director of the Observatory and an expert astronomer, al-Tusi promoted research in all aspects of science, philosophy, mathematics and religious studies. During this period, he composed his masterpiece, 'Astronomical Catalogue of the Ilkhanid ruler'. He dedicated it to Hulagu, his Mongol patron. In addition to this, he authored scores of essays on philosophy, theology, ethics, mathematics and astronomy. In these works, he revised and reformulated the ideas of his predecessors and made considerable advances in arithmetic, trigonometry and geometry.

Most significantly, in the field of astronomy, he proposed a new theory of planetary motion which was different from the Ptolemaic theory. This later inspired Qutb al-Din Shirazi, Ulugh Beg, Ibn al-Shatir and Nicolaus Copernicus to formulate their own theories of planetary motion. Although Copernicus is today considered to be the first person to have formulated the heliocentric theory, there is no doubt that the astronomical ideas of al-Tusi and his successors greatly influenced him.

Indeed, writing on spherical trigonometry, he pointed out in his text, 'The Book of the Quadrilateral', that trigonometry was an independent subject, separate from astronomy. With the publication of this book, he firmly established both planar and spherical trigonometry as distinct branches of mathematics, which later influenced prominent Muslim astronomers and mathematicians like al-Kashi, who was a colleague of Ulugh Beg at the Timurid Observatory in Samarqand. Also, as a powerful practitioner of Peripatetic philosophy, al-Tusi wrote an extensive commentary on Ibn Sina's celebrated philosophical text entitled, 'Exegesis of Remarks and Admonitions'. In this book, he defended Ibn Sina against the charges of heresy levelled at him by prominent scholars like al-Ghazali and Fakhr al-Din al-Razi.

His commentary is rated very highly by Shi'a scholars. This is probably because it is an explanatory work, rather than an original philosophical text which attempts to advocate fresh thoughts. Not surprisingly, many commentaries have been written on this book by prominent Shi'a thinkers, like al-Hilli (b. 1250-d. 1325 CE). As a follower and practitioner of Twelver Shi'ism, al-Tusi wrote frequently on *ithna 'ashari* theology. Indeed, he was one of the first to systematically develop the fundamental tenets of Shi'a beliefs and practices. Of his theological works, 'The Definition of Fundamental Beliefs' is today widely considered to be the summary of Twelver Shi'ism. This book became so popular in Persia that scores of influential Shi'a scholars and theologians, including al-Hilli and al-Jurjani wrote extensive commentaries on it.

However, as a religious scholar and jurist, al-Tusi believed that the public should keep away from engaging in complex theological debates and discussions because, he believed, this could lead to doubts in belief and theological misunderstandings. Only those who were well-versed in the religious sciences were, in his view, qualified to engage in such debate. Instead, he urged the public to fulfil their religious obligations and live their lives according to the *shari'ah* (Islamic law), leaving the responsibility of interpreting and formulating the shari'ah to the *ulama* (religious scholars) and *fuqaha* (jurists). By contrast, his ethical views in his book titled *Kitab al-Akhlaq-i-Nasiri* and in other treatises are both complex and thought-provoking.

Al-Tusi was influenced by the works of Aristotle, al-Farabi, Ibn Miskawayh and Ibn al-Muqaffa. He was also influenced by the ideas of ancient Persian and Indian philosophers and sages. So he developed a comprehensive and universalistic ethical philosophy. The purpose of his ethical philosophy was to nourish and cultivate people's moral and ethical qualities through the continuous pursuit of knowledge. This, he felt, would contribute to the development of good human character and personality. He was keen to promote religious tolerance and cultural harmony. His ethical dialogue sought to unite people of all religious and racial backgrounds based on our common humanity. Although his ethical thinking was not entirely original, it was nevertheless very ambitious and deserves much more recognition, especially in this day and age, than it has so far received.

Like al-Kindi, Abu Bakr al-Razi, Ibn Sina and Ibn Rushd before him, al-Tusi was a great thinker and encyclopaedist but, unlike them, his works did not gain much currency beyond the borders of Persia, perhaps because he wrote primarily in Persian. He authored more than one hundred books and treatises on almost all the sciences of his day. Al-Tusi died at the age of seventy-three during the reign of Abaqa Khan (b. 1234-d. 1282 CE), the son and successor of Hulagu, and was buried in Kazimayn, located on the outskirts of Baghdad.

69

Jalal al-Din Rumi
(b.1207 - d.1273 CE) /
(b.604 - d.672 AH)

The thirteenth century of the Common Era and the seventh century of Islam was a challenging period in Muslim history. Having assumed control of North Africa, the Muslims successfully crossed into Sicily, Gibraltar and southern Spain, before they began to knock on the door of mainland Europe. At the same time, in the subcontinent, Mu'izz al-Din Ghuri became the first native Muslim monarch to rule India. As the Muslims made rapid political progress both in the East and the West, the Mongol army unexpectedly emerged from Asia and ransacked Baghdad, the capital of the Islamic world, leaving behind nothing but death and destruction.

Political setbacks, cultural decline and moral degeneration, combined with petty rivalries between different religious groups, led to intolerance, mutual hatred and animosity across the Muslim world. The core values and principles of Islam were ignored and openly violated in many parts. From the chaos, the towering figure of Rumi emerged to champion the higher values and principles of Islam like never before.

Maulana Jalal al-Din Rumi was born in the city of Balkh (in present-day Afghanistan), which at the time was a part of the Persian province of Khurasan. His family claimed descent from Abu Bakr, the first Caliph of Islam. His grandfather, Husayn ibn Ahmad, and father, Baha al-Din, were famous Islamic scholars of their time. Baha al-Din was such an outstanding Islamic scholar and spiritual figure that he was known as the *sultan al-ulama* (supreme religious authority) of his age. Rumi was brought up in a family of scholars and spiritual guides. His education began at home under the watchful gaze of his learned father who taught him Arabic, Persian, traditional Islamic sciences and poetry during his early years. Since his father was widely admired by the people of Balkh for his intense learning and spiritual achievements, young Rumi joined his father on his travels and in the process he met the leading Islamic scholars of the time.

Rumi was influenced by his father's religious ideas and thoughts. His father was heavily influenced by the teachings of the celebrated al-Ghazali (see chapter 56). As a firm opponent of Neoplatonic thought, al-Ghazali launched a vicious intellectual attack on the thoughts of the leading Islamic philosophers including al-Kindi (see chapter 35), al-Farabi (see chapter 41) and Ibn Sina (see chapter 52). Imam al-Ghazali championed the cause of Islamic traditionalism and Sufi thought and practices. Inspired by al-Ghazali, Baha al-Din became a vocal critic of Islamic philosophy and became a champion of Islamic spirituality, ethics and moral values and practices.

Baha al-Din left Balkh for Nishapur with his whole family in the wake of a looming Mongol invasion. In Nishapur, young Rumi encountered the celebrated poet Farid al-Din Attar, the author of the famous *Mantiq al-Tair* (The Conference of the Birds). He gave him copies of his books and prayed for his family's well-being. From Nishapur, Rumi's family continued their journeying and travelled to Baghdad and Syria, before arriving in Makkah in time for the annual *hajj*.

Rumi's family finally settled in Larinda, a town in Arzinjan, when he was around eighteen years old. Here he married and his son was born a year later. His family stayed in Larinda for a while before moving to Konya, the capital of the Turkish Seljuk dynasty, in 1229 CE. Two years later, Baha al-Din died and Rumi, who was only twenty-four, was suddenly expected to shoulder all his family responsibilities. As a gifted young scholar who was blessed with a powerful imagination and sharp intellect, he soon became one of the prominent scholars of his locality thanks to his vast knowledge and understanding of Islam. Having already studied traditional Islamic sciences under the guidance of his father and his personal tutor, Shaykh Burhan al-Din, he was very keen to pursue advanced training in the Islamic sciences.

Accordingly, he travelled to Halab and Damascus, where he devoted the next seven years of his life to the pursuit of advanced Islamic knowledge. After completing his advanced education, he returned to Konya where he lived with Shaykh Burhan al-Din, his former tutor and mentor. He encouraged Rumi to engage in ascetic and pious practices to attain spiritual purification. He was barely thirty-four when he became widely recognised as an outstanding scholar, a worthy successor to his honourable father. Shortly afterwards he established his own religious school. He delivered regular lectures on *tafsir* (Qur'anic commentary), *fiqh* (Islamic jurisprudence), *Hadith*, and Islamic spirituality, morals and ethics. His lectures became so popular that students came from across Konya to listen to him.

His sermons were based on Islamic theology, jurisprudence and Prophetic *Hadith*. Through these, Rumi encouraged all the locals to take their faith more seriously and bring about personal, as well as collective, reformation to achieve success in this life and salvation in the hereafter. While he was busy lecturing on traditional Islamic sciences, suddenly there appeared a sixty-year-old man who turned his life completely upside down. He was clad in tatty and coarse clothes. This old man was aggressive and possessed a very domineering personality. He was Shams al-Din al-Tabriz, an ascetic Sufi, who had abandoned all material comforts and pleasures of this life in favour of Sufi devotional practices. He originated from the family of Hasan-i-Sabbah, the founder of the notorious neo-Isma'ili Assassin sect. Shams was a remarkable ascetic whose piety and spirituality completely swept Rumi off his feet.

Rumi's lectures on the religious sciences made him very popular throughout Konya. However, after he met with Shams, Rumi resigned from his professorship at the local college and became Shams's full-time student and devotee. As an Islamic theologian, he had previously condemned music as being a blameworthy activity. But now he became obsessed with music, singing and dancing to the utter shock and surprise of the locals. The people could not understand why an outstanding theologian and religious scholar like

Rumi would behave in such a scandalous and rude manner. More importantly, the locals could not understand how an aged mystic like Shams could influence such a learned, restrained and gentle scholar like Rumi into following his ascetic ways. No doubt, Shams was a charismatic figure who, having devoted his entire life to the pursuit of Islamic spirituality, had acquired a powerful moral and spiritual aura which clearly deeply affected Rumi.

In other words, in the person of Shams, he saw what he did not observe in others. This was the luminous light of Divine love, compassion and mercy exemplified at its best. Shams became a mirror in which Rumi could see his own spiritual weaknesses, moral failings and physical frailties like never before. What he saw truly shocked and horrified him. In his obsession with Islamic law, he had overlooked the very substance of Islam. Thus, in the life and spiritual teachings of Shams, he discovered the true meaning and significance of Islam. However, the more his devotion to Shams increased, the more his behaviour became erratic and unpredictable. This led to a huge row between Shams and Rumi's relatives, friends and students. Indeed, they eventually forced Shams out of Konya.

Rumi's separation from Shams made him so depressed and miserable that his son volunteered to go out in search of Shams and bring him back to Konya. He found him in Damascus and returned home with the aged mystic. The locals once again showed him their hostility. Why? Because they felt he had misled and deceived one of their brightest scholars. Rumi, however, did not see things in that way. To him, Shams was the embodiment of purity, peace, spirituality and *ma'rifah* (Divine recognition) and, like him, he too longed to attain the peak of Islamic spirituality. But the people of Konya did not share Rumi's profound love and enthusiasm for Shams. Shams was either forced to leave the city or he may have been murdered, probably by someone close to Rumi.

Either way, Shams suddenly disappeared – never to return again. His disappearance affected the forty-one-year-old Rumi intensely. Indeed, many people thought he had gone 'mad' because he refused to believe that Shams had disappeared. During this period, he became completely obsessed with singing and dancing, which the traditional Islamic scholars considered to be an abhorrent practice. But he found peace, solace and reassurance in Sufi music and dance which, he argued, represented an expression of Divine love and grace in its highest form.

After many years of self-imposed suffering and emotional agony, Rumi eventually came to terms with his separation from Shams thanks to a local goldsmith. One day while he was dancing about in the street, he suddenly stopped upon hearing the rhythmic sound of the goldsmith's hammer. He suddenly regained his balance and composure. The beat of the goldsmith's hammer restored Rumi's physical and intellectual composure. He also began to refocus his spiritual energy in the pursuit of Divine recognition. After thanking the illiterate goldsmith for his timely intervention, he gave up his quest for Shams. Now it became clear to him that he was in reality looking for none other than his own innermost self. So, at the age of fifty-four, he finally attained the inner peace and certainty which he had been seeking for so long.

It was during this period that Rumi composed his remarkable *Mathnavi*. The renowned Persian poet and writer Jami, better known as Mulla Jami, referred to it as the 'Persian Qur'an' due to its superb teachings and wisdom. It took Rumi nearly twelve years to dictate the twenty-five thousand and seven hundred verses to his loyal friend and confidant Husam al-Din. It was originally entitled *Husam Namah* (The Book of Husam). This monumental work later became known as the *Mathnavi*. Before the *Mathnavi*, Rumi composed another book of around thirty-five thousand verses in memory of Shams. In it, he explored different aspects of mystical love, questing and longing. But it was his *Mathnavi* which was destined to leave a permanent mark in the annals of Islamic literature.

As a compilation of mystical teachings, spiritual advice and religious parables in the form of poetry, the central message of the *Mathnavi* was one of universal Divine love. This crossed all artificial boundaries, sectarian denominations and crude cultural constraints. Rumi appealed directly to the very source of mystical love, Allah Almighty, with an overwhelming sense of grace and humility. By doing this, he conveyed his universal message of love, compassion and mercy to all people. His mysticism was a unifying force, one where Divinity and humanity met rather than drifted apart. Through this, he hoped to promote mutual understanding and tolerance and establish peace and harmony between people of all faiths, cultures and traditions.

Since Rumi, like us, lived in an age when greed, anger, hatred and hostility led to considerable chaos, disorder, bloodshed and instability around the world, his message of universal love is as relevant today as it was during his lifetime. Also, as a champion of human freedom and individuality, he constantly stressed the need for the attainment of true peace and liberation by moving closer to Divine proximity. This coming together did not involve an absolute union between the Creator and His creatures. Rather, according to Rumi, it represented the meeting of the lover with the object of his love. Love, argued Rumi, was an innate, cosmic feeling which cannot be experienced except by connecting oneself with the Spirit of the universe. Nor can it be experienced by only the performance of external deeds and actions, devoid of inner meaning and content. This universal message of love, compassion and mercy was, therefore, central to Rumi's mystical philosophy which he explained in a masterly fashion in his vast collection of poetry and odes.

Rumi was thoroughly familiar with Islamic theology and philosophy, but he did not consider himself to be a theologian or philosopher as such. He was essentially a spiritual poet, arguably one of the most influential in history. His *Mathnavi* is today widely considered to be one of the most powerful and imaginative poems of all time. In total, he composed more than seventy thousand verses of poetry in Persian. As the founder of the *mawlawiyyah* Order of Sufism, he must also be considered one of the most influential practitioners of Sufism, along with Abd al-Qadir al-Jilani (see chapter 57), Mu'in al-Din Chishti (see chapter 62), Abul Hasan Ali ibn Abdullah al-Shadhili (see chapter 67) and Baha al-Din Naqshband (see chapter 74).

His followers are known as the 'whirling dervishes' for their love of Sufi music, singing and whirling dance. The members of this *tariqa* have been living in Turkey since the early Ottoman period. Rumi is revered both in the East and the West for his remarkable poetic output. His ideas and thoughts have influenced scores of prominent Islamic scholars, thinkers and poets like Mulla Jami and Sir Muhammad Iqbal (see chapter 96). Today, he has also become one of the most popular and widely read Muslim poets in the West, especially in the United States. Rumi died at the age of sixty-six and was buried in Konya, Turkey.

70

Shaykh Sa'di of Shiraz (b.ca.1210 - d.ca.1291 CE) / (b. 607 - d.689 AH)

The words 'ethics' and 'morality' do not mean the same thing. Ethics means 'ethos and character'. The words 'custom' and 'usage' also fall within the wider definition of ethics. But, the word 'morality' refers to the nature of human action rather than the character of the actor. Ancient Greek moral philosophers like Plato and Aristotle had developed detailed ideas of morality. However the nature of the relationship between the 'actor' and his 'action' remained both unclear and controversial within their ethical principles. After Muslims came into contact with the ancient Greek philosophical and scientific heritage during the eighth and ninth centuries, influential Muslim philosophers like al-Kindi (see chapter 35) and al-Farabi (see chapter 41) developed new ethical principles based on the Islamic worldview.

The works of these early Muslim thinkers laid the foundations for a new science which became known as *ilm al-akhlaq* (the science of ethics). In their search to define the 'common good', the Muslims adopted a different approach to ethics and morality. Thus, some like al-Farabi, Ibn Bajjah (b. 1085-d. 1138) and Ibn Tufayl (see chapter 58), adopted a philosophical approach to ethics. Others, like Imam al-Ghazali (see chapter 56) and Fakhr al-Din al-Razi (see chapter 63), followed a theological approach. Others, like Ibn Taymiyyah (see chapter 72) and Ibn Qayyim al-Jawziyyah (b. 1292-d. 1350 CE), adopted a more religious and textual approach to ethics. However, it was Shaykh Sa'di of Shiraz who became one of the most influential advocates of practical ethics. Indeed, he not only clearly defined the 'common good', but he also played a pivotal role in popularising Islamic morality and ethics.

Muslih al-Din ibn Abdullah Shirazi, better known as Shaykh Sa'di, was born in the Persian city of Shiraz into a middle-class Muslim family. His father, Abdullah, was a civil servant by profession and served the then rulers of Shiraz. When Sa'di was still an infant, his father died, and this forced his family to experience considerable financial hardship. The poverty experienced by Sa'di during his childhood remained fixed in his mind. It was later recalled most vividly in his writings. In desperation, he and his mother sought refuge with an Arab chief who understood their pain and showed sympathy.

Normally, when people face such economic hardship, they try to improve their situation by seeking suitable employment, but Sa'di's mother encouraged her son to continue his studies. Being very serious about learning, young Sa'di used to bury himself in his books rather than go out to play games or have fun with his peers. His devotion to his studies impressed his teachers and this also prompted a local wealthy sponsor to volunteer to pay for his education.

At school he followed the standard curriculum of the day and excelled in his studies; thus, his teachers encouraged him to pursue higher education. Some of the leading centres of Islamic education were in Baghdad, Damascus, Basrah, Nishapur, Hira and Isfahan. Accordingly, he proceeded to Baghdad for his higher education and there he composed many essays and poems on both religious and moral topics. He was around twenty-one at the time. He dedicated these essays to his teacher, Shaykh Shams al-Din, who was a professor of literature at the famous Nizamiyah College in Baghdad. The venerable Shaykh was impressed by the young writer's literary ability and agreed to fund his advanced education at Nizamiyah out of his pocket.

As a limitless seeker of knowledge, Sa'di studied a wide range of subjects including traditional Islamic sciences, philosophy, logic, history, geography, science and *tasawwuf* (Islamic spirituality) at

Nizamiyah College under the guidance of famous professors like Hafiz ibn al-Jawzi and Farah ibn al-Jawahir. As the capital of the Abbasid Caliphate, Baghdad at the time was home to some of the Muslim world's leading scholars and thinkers, who willingly taught knowledge and wisdom to those who were eager to learn. Sa'di thus moved freely in and out of the religious circles of all the prominent scholars of Baghdad and drank deep from the fountain of Islamic knowledge. During his stay in Baghdad, he also encountered the celebrated Sufi sage al-Suhrawardi (b. 1145-d. 1234 CE), the founder of the *suhrawardiyah* Sufi Order, who initiated him into his *tariqa*.

After completing his higher education and mastering several languages in addition to Arabic and Persian (which was his mother tongue), Sa'di eventually returned home to Shiraz. Here, he discovered, to his dismay, how the socio-political situation had become very dangerous and unpredictable.

Indeed, while Sa'di was still in Baghdad, his former sponsor Prince Sa'd ibn Zangi had been overthrown from power by his arch-rival Sultan Ghiyath al-Din Isfahani, who was very suspicious of those who allied themselves with the son of Zangi. To make matters worse, the Mongols were threatening to destroy that whole region. This prompted Sa'di to leave Shiraz and travel in pursuit of knowledge. For the next three decades (from 1226 to 1256 CE), he travelled extensively across the Muslim world and explored the lifestyle, culture, tradition and habits of Muslims and non-Muslims alike. During his travels, he visited Arabia to perform *hajj* and then proceeded to Syria, Egypt and North Africa. In Tripoli, he was captured by the Franks and forced into hard labour, but he was rescued by a well-wisher who married his daughter to him. However, the marriage did not last long because Sa'di found the girl too unreasonable and aggressive for his liking.

From North Africa, he travelled to Turkistan, Afghanistan and India where he met the Hindus for the first time. In India, he visited Punjab, Somnath, Gujarat and Delhi Later, he vividly recorded his experiences of these countries in the form of poetry. From there he travelled to Yemen and Abyssinia (present-day Ethiopia) before proceeding to Makkah to perform yet another pilgrimage. In all, he performed more than a dozen pilgrimages. He freely interacted with people of all races and cultural backgrounds, which enabled him to gain an unrivalled insight into human nature, its weaknesses and shortcomings, as well as its positive aspects.

His advanced training in Islamic theological, philosophical and spiritual sciences, coupled with his three decades of travel across the Muslim world, broadened Sa'di's intellectual horizon. It also enriched his awareness and understanding of the diversity which is so characteristic of the human family. Indeed, his observations and admiration of the vast diversity which represents our humanity inspired him to formulate and champion universal ethics which belonged neither to the East nor to the West. His global ethic was rooted in the timeless line of Divine wisdom. It was all about the 'common good'; the common good of all humanity rather than that of a specific group or nation.

After returning to his native Shiraz in 1256 CE at the age of around sixty-six, he authored most of his books, essays and poetry. Sa'di is considered to be a remarkable example of late blooming. He completed two of his most famous works, namely the *Bustan* (The Fruit Garden) and *Gulistan* (The Rose Garden) after his sixty-fifth birthday. The former was finished in 1257 CE, while the latter was completed in 1258 CE. These years were also some of the most traumatic periods in the history of Islam. While Sa'di was busy writing about the permanent values and principles which are common to all people, highlighting the importance of truth, honesty, wisdom and tolerance in promoting healthy human relationships, the Mongol hordes emerged from Asia and marched into Baghdad.

The Mongol attack on Baghdad was so devastating that it shocked and horrified Muslims and non-Muslims alike. Although Sa'di made no specific reference to the Mongol sack of Baghdad in his works, as a devout Muslim and practising Sufi, he must have been devastated by the brutal nature of the Mongol assault on the seat of the Abbasid Caliphate. When the Mongol advance was eventually stopped in 1260 CE by the Mamluks of Egypt, the entire Muslim world breathed a sigh of relief. Amidst the prevailing social and political chaos, an increasingly frail Sa'di came to enjoy the patronage of Prince Abu Bakr ibn Sa'd, the son and successor of his former supporter, Atabek Sa'd ibn Zangi. He admired this young ruler so much that he dedicated his *Bustan* to him, saying that as long as the sun and the moon continue to rise in the skies, the name of

Abu Bakr ibn Sa'd would be fondly remembered by the readers of his *Bustan*.

Comprising more than four thousand couplets, the *Bustan* is today considered to be one of the most widely read works of Persian poetry. Before Sa'di, Persia had produced some of the most influential and gifted poets of the Muslim world, including Hakim Sana'i, Umar Khayyam (see chapter 55) and Farid al-Din Attar. But with the publication of the *Bustan*, he established his reputation as one of the most polished and ethical poets of the Muslim world. Although steeped in Islamic theology, jurisprudence and spirituality, Sa'di's poetry rises above religious formalism to capture the essence of universal Prophetic wisdom.

That is why theological and dogmatic debates and discussions never interested him. His understanding of Islam was primarily a moral and ethical one. It was underpinned by the universal Qur'anic principles and Prophetic wisdom. He was inspired by the eternal teachings of Islam, so Sa'di's moral philosophy combined religious principles, practical ethics and spirituality to create a comprehensive moral code of behaviour in society.

This moral code was a universal one where the kings, queens, rulers, saints, philosophers, theologians as well as lay people had their roles and responsibilities assigned to them. It was not a code in a legal sense; rather it was a humane, tolerant and all-inclusive code of behaviour. Its foremost objective was the promotion of the 'common good' of all people. In his *Bustan*, Sa'di spoke a universal language – which surpassed formal speech – by addressing the human heart, which he considered to be the mirror of universal truth. That is to say, his moral philosophy sought to connect humankind to Divinity at a practical level, without compromising the sacredness of Allah, nor undermining the humanity of the people. The *Bustan* therefore presents a powerful and compelling explanation of universal moral and ethical teachings, underpinned by the timeless wisdom of the Qur'an and Prophetic wisdom, without in any way overlooking their practical dimensions.

In comparison, Sa'di's *Gulistan* is primarily a lyrical work which consists of interesting, witty and instructive anecdotes, stories and tales which seek to inspire the reader to lead a normal and, equally, moral life inspired by the timeless wisdom of Islam. An optimist by nature and a gifted communicator, he analysed human relationships and behaviour through personal observation. He rejoiced when people exemplified good behaviour and manners but, at the same time, he refused to criticise those who fell short of his high moral and ethical standards. He persevered with such people, knowing only too well that we all have our share of mistakes and misbehaviours. Therefore, he preferred to drop hints and make suggestions to those who fell short of his high ethical standards.

Indeed, he operated like a universal friend who informed people of what they needed to know – and in a language they could all understand – without offending anyone. He was wise and entertaining, and never boring. A reader of the *Gulistan* cannot help but smile, reflect and ponder, and do so without having to stretch themselves either physically or intellectually. If his wit was refreshing and his eloquence breathtaking, then his understanding of human nature and behavioural psychology was precise. Yet, strangely enough, Sa'di claimed to have composed his *Gulistan* in a hurry, with information left over from the *Bustan*.

In short, in his *Bustan* and *Gulistan*, Sa'di managed to capture the very essence of Islamic moral and ethical teachings. In so doing, he helped to popularise the moral and ethical code of Islam as never before. As an Islamic scholar and moralist, he is still very popular in Persia and the subcontinent. But, as a writer and poet, he is considered to be one of the most polished and gifted Muslim poets of all time. So much so that an Iranian is not generally considered to be literate until he learns to quote Sa'di by heart. Originally written in Persian, Sa'di's *Gulistan* and *Bustan* have also been translated into all the prominent languages of the world including English, Arabic, Hindi, Urdu, French, German, Bengali, Russian, Turkish and even Latin.

Unfortunately, his exact age at the time of his death is not known. Some suggest over one hundred, while others say around ninety-nine. Either way, he was laid to rest in his native Shiraz. But his powerful and enduring poetry and moral teachings have continued to influence scholars, writers, poets and lay people alike, both in the East and the West, up to the present time. Indeed, the following couplet from his *Gulistan*, which has also been inscribed on a wall in the Hall of the United Nations, beautifully summarises his entire moral and ethical philosophy:

> All human beings are members of one frame,
> Since all, at first, from the same essence came.
> When time afflicts a limb with pain,
> The other limbs cannot at rest remain.
> If thou feel not for other's misery,
> A human being is no name for thee.

71

Yahya ibn Sharaf al-Nawawi (b.1233 - d.1277 CE) / (b.631 - d.676 AH)

The Qur'an declared the Prophet Muhammad to be the best role model for all people. The need to record his sayings and lifestyle became a major responsibility for his *sahabah* (companions) and early Islamic scholars. These scholars were known as the *muhaddithun* (experts in *Hadith*). They dominated Islamic thought and scholarship from the very beginning. The historians of *Hadith* literature have identified three phases during which the traditionists (*muhaddithun*) made great efforts in the subject of *Hadith*. These periods can be classified as the early, classical, and pre-modern stages.

The early stage comprised the Prophet's companions (*sahabah*) and their successors (*tabiun*). The Prophet's close companions like Abu Hurairah (see chapter 9), Aishah bint Abi Bakr (see chapter 12), and Anas ibn Malik played a crucial role in preserving and spreading the Prophetic *Hadith* in this period. They were supported by their able students like Ibn Shihab al-Zuhri, Sa'id ibn Musayyib, Masruq, Muhammad ibn Sirin and others. These people accurately analysed and protected the Prophetic traditions.

The preservation by this group paved the way for the second stage. In this classical stage, other compilers of *Hadith* emerged and composed their famous collections. These included *Al-Muwatta* of

Malik ibn Anas (see chapter 24), *Al-Musnad* of Ahmad ibn Hanbal (see chapter 31), *Jami al-Sahih* of both al-Bukhari (see chapter 36) and Muslim (see chapter 37) and the *Sunan* of Abu Dawud and others. These traditionists systematically examined thousands of *Hadith* before compiling their celebrated books for the benefit of future generations. After these classical compilers, in the third stage, many prominent scholars of *Hadith* emerged. These included al-Bayhaqi, al-Bagawi, al-Tabrizi and others. But the most famous *muhaddith* of the pre-modern period was al-Nawawi. He played an influential role in popularising the Prophetic traditions.

Imam al-Nawawi's name is Yahya ibn Sharaf al-Damashqi. He was born in the village of Nawa, near Damascus in Syria. He was of Arabian descent. His ancestor had moved to Syria many generations earlier and settled in Nawa. Sharaf ibn Muri, the father of al-Nawawi, was well known in Nawa as a businessman who owned a retail outlet. He was a devout Muslim who practised Sufism. Al-Nawawi was born and raised in a strong Islamic environment. As a result, he developed an instant attraction to Islamic principles and practices.

He was also a hardworking and studious child. He memorised the entire Qur'an before the age of twelve, much to the delight of his father and extended family. Al-Nawawi was blessed with a sharp intellect and strong retentive memory. His father encouraged him to continue his studies rather than join the family business. He attended the local village school and studied Arabic, Qur'an, and some Islamic sciences. He was so studious that he avoided recreational activities and instead read books. When the local children asked him to play games with them, he refused. He said that his studies were more important to him than anything else. His scholarly character and love for learning won him the admiration of the local people. His father was impressed with his achievements. So, after completing his early education, he sent his son to Damascus for further education. He wanted his son to realise his full potential.

Historically speaking, Damascus became a major centre of Islamic learning and education during the early days of Islam. Some of the leading *sahabah* of the Prophet settled there to pursue business and teach Islamic knowledge. Then, during the Umayyad period, the city became the seat of the Caliphate and the dazzling capital of the Islamic world. It also became the outstanding centre of Islamic learning, culture, and civilisation. Thus, it attracted some of the finest scholars, thinkers, and writers of the Muslim world. By the thirteenth century, Damascus had lost much of its former glory. But it still retained its position as one of the Muslim world's leading centres of learning. At the time, some of the most famous scholars of the Qur'an, *Hadith*, *fiqh* (Islamic jurisprudence) and *tasawwuf* (spirituality) lived and taught there.

Damascus boasted that it had no fewer than three hundred religious seminaries and colleges. They taught both religious and scientific subjects. The rulers and well-known religious figures sponsored these schools. Al-Nawawi moved to Damascus and enrolled at *madrasah al-rawahiyah* for his intermediate and advanced education. He was eighteen. This *madrasah* was generously financed by Ibn Rawah, a wealthy Damascene trader. Al-Nawawi first studied medicine before switching over to traditional Islamic sciences. For two years, he studied Arabic grammar, *Hadith*, and Islamic jurisprudence, especially *Shafi'i* legal thought. He studied under the guidance of many distinguished scholars.

His time at *Madrasah al-rawahiyah* was both challenging and very fruitful. On a personal level, he studied with utmost dedication. He slept only a few hours at night. He ate most sparingly and often survived only on biscuits and water. He read intensively until a combination of tiredness and sleeplessness forced him to take a short nap. He studied twelve subjects daily. These include *Hadith*, grammar, *mantiq* (logic), and jurisprudence. He would not take a break until he had thoroughly researched and taken extensive notes on all subjects. His physical patience, eye for detail and devotion to his studies soon won him much praise in both Damascus and his native Nawa.

According to the scholar al-Dhahabi, Imam al-Nawawi was gifted with an unusual ability to focus on his studies. This enabled him to remain engaged in his research for long periods without the distraction of worldly affairs. He accompanied his father to Makkah to perform the sacred pilgrimage after completing his education at *Madrasah al-rawahiyah*. On his return, he resumed his studies. Like his father, al-Nawawi was influenced by *tasawwuf* (Sufism). He practised self-discipline and *zuhd* (abstinence). His spirituality and practices were influenced more by the Sunnah than by any other considerations. He led a simple and austere lifestyle. He showed no interest in the material possessions of this world. He even refused the offer of an annual wage as a headteacher in Damascus. His main occupation in life was to search for and teach knowledge. He carried out this task with due diligence and great determination. Consequently, his fame spread far and wide. He was unrivalled and a master of *Hadith* literature as well as a leading authority on *fiqh* (Islamic jurisprudence).

It is important to note that he was living in thirteenth-century Damascus. This means he was aware of the challenges that the Muslim world faced at the time. The signs of Islamic political and intellectual decline were clear for all to see. The disputing Muslim rulers of the time failed to resolve their differences and work together to stop the rot. This sad situation continued until the Mongol army appeared from Asia like a thunderbolt from the heavens and destroyed Baghdad. It was the political capital of the Muslim world in 1258 CE. Now the Mongols threatened to overthrow Syria and Egypt as well. With the Mongol threat looming on the horizon, the Mamluk rulers of Syria and Egypt were forced to gather their forces and face the Mongols. This was at the Battle of *Ayn Jalut* (the Spring of Goliath) in 1260 CE. They inflicted a crushing defeat on the Mongols. The Mamluks saved Syria and Egypt from the destruction that had fallen upon Baghdad two years earlier.

When the news of the Mamluk victory reached the public, the whole of Syria erupted in joy. At the time, al-Nawawi was living in Damascus. He too must have joined the people of Syria in their thanksgiving celebrations. Rukn al-Din Baibars, the Turkish Mamluk commander who led the charge against the Mongol forces, was later crowned the fourth Mamluk Sultan of Syria and Egypt. He became a staunch defender of the Islamic East. Sultan Baibars was a gifted commander and military strategist. But he was far from being a generous and sympathetic ruler. He surrounded himself with much wealth and luxury. He forced the poor to pay for his military expeditions.

On one occasion, when the Sultan was short of money, he called all the prominent scholars of Syria to a meeting. He asked them to sign a fatwa (legal decree) which declared that it was a religious obligation for the locals to contribute to the cost of his military expeditions. As a leading scholar of Damascus, al-Nawawi also attended this meeting. But he flatly refused to sign the decree. He argued that it was unfair to impose more taxes on the poor, while the Sultan and his courtiers had surrounded themselves with so much wealth and luxury. His refusal shocked and surprised everyone present at the royal court. After he left, the Sultan was asked why he did not punish him. He replied that al-Nawawi's presence filled him with fear and awe.

Al-Nawawi was a brave scholar. He was also a man of sound principles and practices. As a great scholar of Islamic jurisprudence and *Hadith*, he practised what he preached. He never failed to stand up for what he considered to be right, just and fair. In addition to the serious political problems of the time, al-Nawawi was deeply disturbed by the moral, ethical, and spiritual downfall which threatened to devastate the Muslim world at the time. He thus devoted all his time and energy to composing books on *Hadith*, Islamic jurisprudence, biographical studies, grammar and *tasawwuf*. He composed around sixty books and treaties. His most popular and influential works include *Riyad al-Salihin* (The Garden of the Righteous), *Al-Minhaj fi Sharh Sahih Muslim ibn al-Hajjaj* (A voluminous commentary of *Sahih Muslim*), *Bustan al-'Arifin* (Garden of Gnostics) and *Kitab al-Arba'in* (The Book of Forty *Hadith*).

The *Riyad as-Salihin* is a unique and very accessible anthology of Prophetic traditions. He composed it for scholars and laypeople alike. It consists of more than three hundred and fifty sections. This remarkable book contains guidance from the Qur'an and *Hadith* covering all aspects of life. He thoroughly studied *Hadith* literature including the famous books of al-Bukhari, Muslim, Abu Dawud, al-Tirmidhi, al-Nasa'i and Ibn Majah. He then produced his anthology by drawing information from only authentic sources. Not surprisingly, the *Riyad as-Salihin* is rated very highly by Islamic scholars. It has also been translated and published in all the prominent languages of the world.

In addition to this, al-Nawawi wrote commentaries on *Sahih al-Bukhari* and *Sunan Abu Dawud*. But his commentary on *Sahih Muslim* is one of the best written on that collection of *Hadith*. It has now been translated into English. He also produced a summary of *Sunan al-Tirmidhi*. But his most popular and influential work is *Kitab al-Arba'in*. Like his *Riyad as-Salihin*, this small collection of forty *Hadith* has been translated into all the main languages of the world, including Persian, Urdu, Hindi, Bengali, French, and English.

Besides his remarkable contributions to *Hadith* literature, Imam al-Nawawi was one of the most respected explainers of Shafi'i jurisprudence along with Ibn Hajar al-Asqalani and Taj al-Din al-Subki. He wrote countless books on Prophetic traditions, biographical studies, jurisprudence and Islamic spirituality to revive and popularise the Prophetic practices at a time when the Muslim world was becoming increasingly detached from its Islamic roots.

Al-Nawawi lived in Damascus for more than twenty-five years. He studied, taught, and authored all his books during this period. Most interestingly, he did not marry despite being a strict follower of the Prophetic *Sunnah*. In 1277 CE, he returned all the books he had borrowed from his friends and left Damascus for Jerusalem. He performed prayers at the *Masjid al-aqsa* (Farthest Mosque). He also visited the tomb of Prophet Ibrahim in Hebron, before returning home to Nawa.

Soon after his arrival, he passed away at the age of forty-five. His father was still alive at the time of his death. He was buried in Nawa where a tomb was later erected as a tribute to his memory. The anthologies of *Hadith* he composed continue to be read and studied by millions of people across the globe to this day.

72

Ibn Taymiyyah
(b.1263 - d.1328 CE) /
(b.662 - d.729 AH)

'Back to the Qur'an and *Sunnah*' is a famous slogan which has been used by Muslim scholars and reformers throughout Islamic history to invite disobedient Muslim rulers and the public back to the original, pure Islam as taught by the Prophet Muhammad. The call worked due to the Muslim belief that the Qur'an is Allah's final communication to humanity and the *Sunnah* of the Prophet provides a powerful and valid commentary on the Divine revelation. In other words, these two sources combined to provide an effective method for living a truly Islamic life. For this reason, Muslim scholars and reformers have been able to repeatedly use this slogan successfully throughout Islamic history. *Shaykh al-Islam* Ibn Taymiyyah was one such extraordinary scholar and reformer whose religious thoughts have continued to apply a powerful influence on Muslims up to the present day.

Taqi al-Din Ahmad ibn Abd al-Halim, famously known as Ibn Taymiyyah was born in Harran, a city around Damascus, into a distinguished family of writers, scholars and theologians. His father, Abd al-Halim, and grandfather, Majd al-Din, were highly praised *Hanbali fuqaha* (jurists) who had authored numerous books on *fiqh* (Islamic jurisprudence) and *Hadith*. Brought up in an intellectually friendly environment, Ibn Taymiyyah memorised the entire Qur'an and received training in Arabic language, grammar, *Hadith* and aspects of *fiqh* under the guidance of his learned father.

When he was only seven, his entire family was forced to flee from Harran due to the threat of a Mongol attack on the city. The Mongol stormed out of Asia like a thunderbolt from the heavens. They inflicted a crushing blow on the Muslim world by invading Baghdad, the seat of the Abbasid Caliphate. They destroyed everything before them with unspeakable brutality; at the time the entire Muslim world was gripped by fear. The Mongol invasion of Baghdad represented one of the most destructive periods in Islamic history, but it was the heroic Egyptian Mamluk soldiers who finally stopped them at the Battle of *ayn jalut* (the 'Spring of Goliath'). The Mamluk victory at *ayn jalut* saved Egypt, Arabia and the neighbouring Islamic lands from Mongol invasion and looting.

Ibn Taymiyyah's family were not prepared to take risks so they moved to the safety of Damascus, which was then controlled by the victorious Mamluks. In Damascus, Ibn Taymiyyah's family received a warm welcome from the locals as well as the city's governor. Because of his scholarly and literary accomplishments, his father was appointed the principal of a local *dar al-uloom* (Islamic seminary), where he delivered regular lectures on traditional Islamic sciences. When his name and fame began to spread across Damascus, he was invited to deliver regular *kutbah* (sermons) at the city's historic Umayyad mosque. Like his father and grandfather, young Ibn Taymiyyah was an exceptionally bright student who was blessed with a sharp intellect and retentive memory. Unsurprisingly, he easily memorised vast quantities of information including the whole Qur'an, large collections of *Hadith*, fatwa (juristic rulings), poetry and books on philosophy and logic.

His remarkable retentive power aside, Ibn Taymiyyah was a wide-ranging reader who studied books on *tafsir* (Qur'anic commentary), *kalam* (theology), Islamic jurisprudence and philosophy quicker than an average person could eat their dinner. His thirst for knowledge was such that he claimed to have studied under no fewer than two hundred distinguished Islamic scholars of his day, including al-Maqdisi, who was the Chief Justice of Damascus. Along with his father, Abd al-Halim, and uncle, Fakhr al-Din, he was one of the most respected scholars of *tafsir*, *Hadith* and *fiqh* in

Damascus at the time. He sat at the feet of these great personalities and thoroughly mastered traditional Islamic sciences. So much so that Shams al-Din, the Chief Justice, considered Ibn Taymiyyah to be competent enough to issue fatwa (juristic rulings) when he was barely seventeen years old.

Ibn Taymiyyah's formal education was that of a *Hanbali* theologian and jurist. He was also very fond of the Qur'an from the start. He spent hours on end studying and meditating on the meaning of the Qur'anic *suwar* (chapters) and *ayat* (verses). He even claimed to have read more than two hundred different *tafsir* (commentaries) of the Qur'an to familiarise himself with the diversity of views on Qur'anic scholarship.

Indeed, Ibn Taymiyyah's reading was nothing short of astonishing in its breadth and scope. He covered all aspects of theology, Sufi thought, Islamic history, heresy literature, comparative religion and Greek philosophy and logic as interpreted and championed by Muslim philosophers like al-Farabi (see chapter 41) and Ibn Sina (see chapter 52). After conducting extensive research in almost all the branches of learning of his time, he became recognised as a multitalented Islamic scholar and all-around thinker. Following the death of his father, he was appointed professor of Islamic Thought at the same institution where his father once taught. He was only twenty at the time. According to the historian al-Dhahabi, Ibn Taymiyyah ate very little; he had no more than a few clothes and was devoid of sexual passion, thus he remained a confirmed bachelor all his life.

He was still in his twenties when Ibn Taymiyyah's fame began to spread far and wide. Then, in 1292 CE, he went to Makkah to perform the sacred *hajj*. After completing the *hajj*, he returned to Damascus where he began to lecture at the city's grand Umayyad mosque. Being an inspirational and thought-provoking speaker, his lectures attracted people from all around. His ability to recall Qur'anic verses and Prophetic traditions with ease made him very popular with the people of Damascus. They flocked to the mosque in their thousands to hear him speak. However, his growing fame and popularity made some local theological and political elites very angry and jealous.

Since Ibn Taymiyyah was very outspoken, these people hated him, and they wanted him thrown out of Damascus. He was thirty-five when the first of a series of unfortunate incidents took place which became a source of misery and hardship for him. He was not only keen on preaching, he also issued fatwa (legal rulings) on several controversial theological issues. This infuriated the established scholars of Damascus who called on the local authorities to punish him for alleged heresy and deviation. The authorities were eager to suppress the uproar. So, they complied with the scholars' demands and imprisoned Ibn Taymiyyah.

As a gifted scholar, Ibn Taymiyyah challenged intellectual categorisation. He was brought up and educated as a *Hanbali* theologian and jurist but he pushed the boundaries of the existing theological and legal thought to their limits. He was not attracted to Ash'arism nor Mu'tazilism. On the contrary, he passionately disproved both theologies. He preferred to interpret Islamic beliefs and concepts by following the method of the *salaf al-salih* (pious predecessors). This was based on a literalist understanding of the Qur'an, *Hadith*, sayings of the *Sahaba* (Prophet's companions) and their *tabiun* (successors). Despite being a *Hanbali* jurist, he refused to follow exclusively any one of the four main *madhahib* (schools of Islamic legal thought). This left him wide open to accusations of deviation and religious *bida* (innovation).

Instead of taqlid (imitating) one of the existing *madhahib*, he used his *ijtihad* (intellectual judgement). By doing this, he attempted to develop a fresh understanding of the Islamic scriptural sources, especially if he felt the views of the existing schools contradicted the original Islamic sources. However, unlike what some of his so-called followers say today, he did not reject the existing *madhahib* totally. As a *mujtahid* (one who was qualified to practice *ijtihad*), he felt he was not duty-bound to follow any one of the existing schools of law. That is why he developed his own interpretation and understanding of Islamic theology and jurisprudence. Not surprisingly, his attempts to analyse and interpret the Qur'an, Prophetic *Hadith* and the views of the early Muslims in the light of his own condition met with stiff opposition from the established *ulama* (religious scholars) of Damascus.

Being uncompromising and at times stubborn, Ibn Taymiyyah rarely backed down in a confrontation with his opponents. On one occasion, when he was asked to explain *al-Asma wa'l Sifat Allah* (the divine Names and Attributes) in the light of the Qur'an and

Prophetic traditions, he provided a detailed answer to the question. But his critics accused him of anthropomorphism. During this period, he engaged in regular controversial debates with his opponents until the Mongol army unexpectedly breached the heavily fortified defences erected by the Mamluks and occupied Syria. In response, Ibn Taymiyyah urged the people of Damascus to engage in *jihad* (military struggle) and liberate their country from Mongol occupation. His declaration of *jihad* so inspired the Syrian people that they took up arms to repel the invaders.

Impressed by Ibn Taymiyyah's ability to rally the masses as well as the troops, the governor of Damascus requested that he go to Cairo and ask the Mamluk Sultan Nasir al-Din Muhammad to assist the Syrians in their battle against the Mongols. Sultan Nasir was moved by Ibn Taymiyyah's appeal for help and agreed to support the Syrian people. Thanks to Ibn Taymiyyah, a combined Egyptian-Syrian army confronted the Mongols and in the ensuing battle, he fought like a lion until the enemy was driven out of Mamluk territories. While Ibn Taymiyyah was busy fighting fearlessly on the battlefield, his critics were nowhere to be seen. Indeed, some of them even fled the battlefield as soon as they saw the advancing enemy.

His role in the war against the Mongols won him national recognition in Syria. His critics were angered by the heroic reception granted to him by the Syrian people. So they began to conspire against him once again. Their hatred of Ibn Taymiyyah's thorough theological and legal thinking, coupled with his newfound fame and popularity with the Syrian people and the reigning Sultan (who regularly consulted him on both the political and religious issues of the day), prompted them to engage in religious and political debate to undermine his political and religious standing. Ibn Taymiyyah was not only an open opponent of those who practised *taqlid* in matters of law, he went out of his way to expose what he considered to be the unorthodox beliefs and practices of the Sufis, especially the metaphysical thought of Ibn al-Arabi (see chapter 65).

He also attacked philosophers like al-Farabi (see chapter 41), Ibn Sina (see chapter 52), Fakhr al-Din al-Razi (see chapter 63) and even questioned some of al-Ghazali's theological views (see chapter 56). Moreover, he comprehensively rejected Christian views about Jesus. He also systematically refuted the beliefs and practices of many other religious groups and sects. His intellectual brilliance, coupled with his extensive study of Islamic thought, philosophy, logic and comparative religion, enabled him to analyse and evaluate the beliefs and practices of all of these groups in the light of the Qur'an and Prophetic *Sunnah.* After that, he openly pronounced his verdicts on them, something which earned him the anger of the ruling elites.

His main mission in life was to purify Islamic beliefs and practices from the grip of *bida* (blameworthy innovation) and *shirk* (associationism). Ibn Taymiyyah remained very firm and uncompromising in his efforts to revive the Prophetic practices. His stance on various religious issues led to his imprisonment on several occasions. However, he suffered these trials and ordeals with patience and perseverance. His spells in prison proved intellectually very productive because it was during these periods that he wrote most of his books.

As an undisputed master of traditional Islamic sciences and a prolific writer, according to al-Dhahabi, he authored around one hundred books and treatises on Islamic sciences, comparative religion, philosophy, logic and mysticism. According to his other biographers, he authored as many as five hundred books and essays on a wide range of subjects. His most famous books include *Minhaj al-Sunnah al-Nabawiyah* (Towards Prophetic Methodology) and 'Public Duties in Islam'. He also authored a forty-volume commentary on the Qur'an, but this has not survived.

Ibn Taymiyyah died in prison at the age of sixty-five. When the news of his death was relayed across Damascus, the people of the city came out in great numbers to mourn his death. It is not possible to exaggerate Ibn Taymiyyah's influence and greatness. He is considered to be one of the Muslim world's greatest thinkers, ideologues and warriors. His religious ideas have inspired generations of outstanding Islamic scholars, thinkers and reformers like Muhammad ibn Abd al-Wahhab (see chapter 85), Shah Waliullah (see chapter 86), Muhammad Abduh (see chapter 92), Abul A'la Mawdudi (see chapter 101) and Hasan al-Banna (see chapter 103), among others.

73

Ibn Battuta
(b.1304 - d.1378 CE) /
(b.704 - d.780 AH)

Muhammad ibn Ahmad ibn Jubayr (b. 1145-d. 1217 CE) was not only one of the Muslim world's most prominent explorers, but he was also one of the great travellers of medieval Europe. He left Islamic Spain and travelled across the Islamic East (including Egypt, Arabia and Syria) before finally returning home to record his views and experiences of those lands in the form of memoirs which later became famous both in the East and the West.

After a hundred years, Marco Polo (b. 1254-d. 1324 CE), the celebrated Venetian merchant and adventurer, travelled extensively across Europe and Asia. In addition to Baghdad, he visited China where he reportedly served the famous Mongol ruler, Kublai Khan, for a period before returning to Venice. He later wrote a detailed account of his travels which continues to be read widely to this day. Both Ibn Jubayr and Marco Polo were great travellers who undertook their journeys at a time when long-distance travelling was not normal. A year after Marco Polo's death, a young North African Muslim set out to discover the world, travelling a significant part of the then-known world on foot, riding on mules and sailing on boats, and in so doing he became arguably the greatest traveller in human history. This fearless, tough and inspirational explorer was none other than the influential, Ibn Battuta.

Muhammad ibn Abdullah al-Luwati, better known as Ibn Battuta, was born in Tangier (in present-day Morocco) into a distinguished family of Islamic scholars and judges. Although his ancestors originally originated from the outskirts of Egypt, his family members later became prominent figures of the Berber tribe of Luwata. He was brought up and educated in a learned and wealthy family. Ibn Battuta studied Arabic language, literature and traditional Islamic sciences during his early years. Since his father and uncles were notable Islamic scholars and prominent members of the local judiciary, he also received advanced training in *fiqh* (Islamic jurisprudence).

Encouraged by his father to follow in his footsteps and become a lawyer, Ibn Battuta completed his formal education in the religious sciences, focusing on Islamic jurisprudence, before he decided to go to Makkah to perform the pilgrimage. Only twenty-one at the time, he was nonetheless very keen to undertake the long and demanding journey to Makkah to accomplish the fifth pillar of Islam and also pursue higher education in Islamic jurisprudence, presumably to enhance his chances of obtaining an important judicial post on his return to Tangier.

In 1325 CE, he bade farewell to his family and set out for Makkah. In those days, journeys from North Africa to Arabia were undertaken by caravan, and often took several months and were always fraught with danger and hardship. The brave and determined Ibn Battuta set out on his own. From Tangier, he travelled to Tilimsan and from there he went to Algiers in the company of a group of merchants. Passing by Constantine, he reached Tunis just in time for the Islamic festival of *Eid al-fitr*. On his arrival, he fell ill but, luckily, he soon recovered. He then discovered that the people of Tunis were preparing their pilgrim caravans. When he approached them to request passage with them, they nominated him to lead the caravans to Makkah, presumably because he had superior knowledge of Islamic principles.

After reaching Tripoli (in present-day Libya), he married for the first time, but the marriage soon ended in divorce, owing to a dispute between Ibn Battuta and his father-in-law. Undeterred by this bad experience, he then married for a second time and celebrated the occasion with a lavish banquet. In April 1326 CE, he arrived in Alexandria with the pilgrim caravans and met a Sufi dervish (Islamic sage) who prophesied that he would one day travel across the world.

Before Ibn Battuta's encounter with the Sufi, he had no intention to travel anywhere other than Makkah and Madinah, but now the idea of travelling and exploring the world really fascinated him. Keen to complete the pilgrimage, he left Alexandria by boat and arrived in Cairo. He toured Cairo and also provided a detailed survey and description of this historic city. He liked what he saw and decided to continue travelling. From Cairo, he travelled across the barren desert and visited Gaza, Hebron, Bethlehem and Jerusalem. During his stay in Jerusalem, Ibn Battuta visited *Masjid al-Aqsa* (The Furthest Mosque) and the Dome of the Rock (*Qubbat al-Sakhra*), which is the Muslim world's third holiest site. He was overwhelmed by the mosque's great beauty and grandeur.

After touring Palestine, he proceeded to Syria, visiting Aleppo and Antioch, before finally arriving in Damascus in August 1326 CE. Like his illustrious predecessor Ibn Jubayr, he found Damascus to be an extremely beautiful city. He stayed in Damascus for a period and attended the lectures of its leading scholars. As a keen student of Islam, he soon obtained *ijaza* (certification) in the traditional Islamic sciences. Here he also married for the third time. But a month later, he left Damascus and set out for Madinah, the city of the Prophet, via Tabuk. As soon as he reached Madinah, he went straight to the Prophet's mosque to pay homage to the blessed Prophet and his close companions, Abu Bakr al-Siddiq (see chapter 3) and Umar ibn al-Khattab (see chapter 6).

After four days of prayer and devotion, he went to Makkah to perform another pilgrimage. With great joy and happiness, he completed all the rites of the pilgrimage. Then, in November 1326 CE, he left Makkah by caravan and soon reached Iraq. After touring all the prominent Iraqi cities, including Najaf, Basrah, Baghdad, Kufah, Mosul and parts of southern Persia, he again returned to Makkah accompanied by a caravan of pilgrims. During his stay in Makkah, he devoted much of his time to prayer and devotional activities and completed his third successive pilgrimage.

A year later, he performed his fourth pilgrimage and obtained certification in advanced Islamic studies. Having chosen not to return home to Tangier, Ibn Battuta decided to travel around the world. Still only twenty-six years old at the time, he left Makkah and sailed to Yemen where he visited both Sana and Aden, before proceeding to Oman. He found this country very fertile and full of trees, plants and all kinds of fruits and vegetables. From Oman, he moved to Hormuz and Bahrain and eventually returned to Makkah in time for his fifth pilgrimage in 1332 CE. After completing the pilgrimage, he decided to go to India and see the land of Sultan Muhammad ibn Tughluq for the very first time.

From Makkah, he went to Yemen, hoping to get on a ship bound for India. During his previous trip to Yemen, the locals had told him that thoroughbred horses were regularly shipped to India from Yemen and this, no doubt, encouraged him to board a ship to India. However, his plans failed and instead, he was forced to take the difficult route to Ladhiqiya via Cairo, Syria and the Palestinian cities of Gaza, Hebron and Jerusalem. Here he was fortunate to board a Genoese vessel destined for the ancient Turkish region of Anatolia. After ten days and ten nights at sea, an exhausted Ibn Battuta eventually arrived in Anatolia, where he received a warm welcome from the locals, despite not being able to speak a word of Turkish.

From Anatolia, he proceeded to Konya, where the mausoleum of Mawlana Jalal al-Din Rumi (see chapter 69), the great Sufi and poet, had become an important centre of Sufi activities. From Konya, he continued his journey towards Amasya where he celebrated the annual Islamic festival of *Eid al-adha* in the distinguished company of its governor. Then he headed in the direction of the Caucasus, the land of Sultan Muhammad Uzbeg Khan of the Golden Horde. But the bitterly cold and harsh environment of the Caucasus prompted him to proceed to the capital of Greater Bulgaria, and from there he went to the ancient city of Constantinople (present-day Istanbul) in the company of Sultan Muhammad Uzbeg Khan's wife. Unlike his stay in the Caucasus, his time in Constantinople proved very fruitful, not least because he was able to tour the whole city and provide an elaborate survey and description of what he saw.

However, according to some historians, he may not have visited all the places he mentioned in his *Rihla* (Travels), although no serious reader of, for example, his description of Sarai, the capital of the Tatar dynasty, can help but feel that they are reading anything but an eye-witness account of that place. Furthermore, Ibn

Battuta's accounts of his travels in Asia Minor have been proven and corroborated by other historical sources. So, from Sarai, he travelled through Khwarizm, Khiva, Bukhara, Samarqand and Balkh before he reached the historic province of Khurasan. From here, he went to Kabul, the capital of modern Afghanistan, and in September 1333 CE, at the age of twenty-nine, he finally reached the borders of India. After crossing the Indus River, he went to Multan where he received a warm welcome from its governor. From there, he set out for Delhi, the magnificent capital of Muslim India, where he joined the reigning Sultan's civil service. However, given his superior education and extensive knowledge of Islamic law, the ruling elites within the Sultan's government became very jealous of him and began to conspire against him.

He stayed in India for a long time and travelled extensively across the country. He closely observed the local people, their culture, customs and habits. Other than al-Biruni (see chapter 50), the Muslim astronomer and scientist (who composed his famous 'History of India' during his long stay in India), no other medieval traveller or writer had provided such a detailed description of India as Ibn Battuta. According to Ibn Khaldun (see chapter 75), the great historian of Islam, his accounts of India were so detailed, bewildering and adventurous that, on his return to Morocco, he received a mixed reaction at the court of Sultan Abu Inan.

Although he may have slightly overstated his adventures in India, even a critical historian like Ibn Khaldun did not question the authenticity of his travel accounts, which have also been substantiated by other reliable historical Indian sources. After almost a decade in India, just as Ibn Battuta finally decided to return to Makkah, the reigning Sultan summoned him to his court and requested him to head a diplomatic mission to the Mongol ruler of China. Keen to undertake yet another adventure, he accepted the Sultan's offer and set out for the Far East.

The journey through mainland India was filled with many dangers and difficulties. On one occasion he was taken prisoner by local tribesmen but fortunately managed to escape unharmed. After reaching Calicut, he embarked on a Chinese vessel but as soon as he boarded the vessel it sank, leaving him stranded on the shore. Eventually, he reached the Maldives Islands, where he stayed for eighteen months, married for the fourth time, and also worked as a *qadi* (judge), before proceeding to Ceylon (modern Sri Lanka). Ibn Battuta's description of the Maldives Islands is today considered to be one of the most detailed and illuminating travel accounts of all time.

No other writer or traveller has been able to surpass his description and account of these stunning islands and their people. In Ceylon, he toured the country and even climbed its highest mountain, commonly known as 'Adam's Footprint', before he sailed to Chittagong and Sylhet in East Bengal (in present-day Bangladesh) where he spent three days with Shaykh Jalal al-Din ibn Muhammad, better known as Shah Jalal. From East Bengal, he travelled to the Indonesian island of Sumatra and there boarded a vessel which took him on to China. According to Ibn Battuta, China was a beautiful country, and he found the Chinese people very kind and courteous, but, as a practising Muslim, he found their eating habits repulsive; he noted, to his disgust, how the Chinese were very fond of pork.

Although Ibn Battuta stayed in China for only a short period, he observed Chinese culture, customs and habits first-hand. From China, he returned to Sumatra and from there he went on to Malabar. Now in his mid-forties, he finally decided to head westwards. Travelling along the Persian Gulf, he soon reached Baghdad and from there he went to Syria where, for the first time, he witnessed the havoc wreaked by the deadly plague known as 'the Black Death'. From Syria, he went via Egypt to Makkah, to perform yet another pilgrimage. After completing the pilgrimage, he again returned to Egypt to sail from Alexandria to Tunis, and from there he took a ship to Algiers and reached his native Morocco in November 1349 CE.

After travelling around the world, in 1352 CE, at the age of forty-eight, he embarked on yet another adventure. He crossed the Strait of Gibraltar and arrived in Granada. From there, he returned to Morocco and crossed the Saharan desert to spend some time with the Muslim Mandingos in Niger. There, he was surprised to discover that the locals constructed their houses with rock salt. Today, his travel accounts of Niger and Timbuktu are an invaluable source of medieval African history and culture. Ibn Battuta eventually returned to Fez at the age of fifty and by royal order, he dictated his *Rihla* (Accounts of Travel) to Sultan Abu Inan's personal secretary, Ibn Juzayy al-Kalbi, under the title of 'A Gift to Observers, Dealing with the Curiosities of Cities and the Wonder of Travels'.

Ibn Battuta spent the next twenty-four years of his life in Fez. During this period, he also served as a judge and eventually died at the age of seventy-four or in his mid-sixties. Known widely as the 'Traveller of Islam', he travelled more than seventy-five thousand miles and did so all on his own. He achieved this unprecedented feat at a time when long-distance travel was far from being straight-forward or free from peril. As such, it would not be an exaggeration to say that he was one of the great pioneers of international travel and cultural reporting.

Indeed, his record of seventy-five thousand miles remained unbeaten until steam engines were invented in the eighteenth century. Thanks to Sir Hamilton A. R. Gibb (b. 1895-d. 1971 CE), the renowned British Arabist, his entire *Rihla* is now available in English. An abridged edition published in 1929 CE under the title of *The Travels of Ibn Battuta*, continues to be read widely to this day.

74

Khwajah Naqshband (b.1317 - d.1389 CE) / (b.718 - d.792 AH)

Although the Muslims first entered Central Asia during the reign of Caliph Umar, the Islamic presence in that region was not established until the time of Caliph Uthman. The Muslim conquest of Central Asia paved the way for a strongly Islamic culture and identity to emerge in that region. So much so that Central Asia produced some of the Muslim world's most influential scholars, thinkers and personalities, like al-Khwarizmi (see chapter 32), al-Bukhari (see chapter 36), Ibn Sina (see chapter 52), al-Maturidi and Ulugh Beg. Amir Timur (Tamerlane), was one of the most successful conquerors in history. He was also born and raised on the cold, harsh and intimidating plains of Central Asia. Amir Timur was known for his thirst for power and military conquest, but this fearless military hardman had a soft spot for *tasawwuf* (Islamic spirituality). This is hardly surprising because Central Asia had produced some of the Muslim world's most famous and influential Sufi sages.

Indeed, Sufism became part and parcel of the Central Asian religious scene during the early days of Islam. Thus, outstanding early Central Asian Sufis like Abu Sa'id ibn Abul Khayr of Mayhana (in present-day Turkmenistan) played a vital role in the development of a unique Central Asian Sufi identity. Thanks to them, many local *tariqa* (Islamic spiritual traditions) emerged and became established in that region during the thirteenth and fourteenth centuries. One such Sufi tradition was the *naqshbandiyah tariqa*, which was championed by Kawajah Naqshband. It is today widely considered to be one of the Muslim world's most influential Sufi traditions.

Muhammad ibn Muhammad Baha al-Din, better known as Khwajah Naqshband, was born in the village of Qasr-i Hinduwan, near Bukhara in modern Uzbekistan in Central Asia. When he was a child, he was blessed by Muhammad Baba Sammasi, a famous local spiritual figure. He foretold that the young boy would one day become a shining star of Islamic spirituality. After completing his early education in traditional Islamic sciences and Sufism under the guidance of Baba Sammasi, Khwajah Naqshband, travelled to Bukhara to pursue higher education. During his stay in Bukhara, he married and eventually returned home after completing his formal studies.

He then went to Nasaf where Sayyid Amir Kulal, a prominent scholar and spiritual successor of Baba Sammasi, lived and taught Islamic sciences and spirituality. Born in a local village, Sayyid Kulal earned his living as a potter but had become a leading promoter of Islamic spirituality. Under Sayyid Kulal's guidance, Khwajah Naqshband mastered Sufi thought and practices.

After Sayyid Kulal's death, his mantle passed to his able disciple, Mawlana Arif Dikkarani. Khwajah Naqshband served Mawlana for another few years before he went to Samarqand where he entered the service of the reigning Sultan Khalil. He served him for twelve years until the Sultan was overthrown from power in 1347 CE. During this period of considerable social and political uncertainty, Khwajah Naqshband moved to Ziwartun where he received advanced training in Sufi theory and practice.

Known for his good character, personal piety and holiness, the Khwajah soon became a well-known religious figure. The locals rated him highly for his knowledge of Islam and his spiritual qualities. His advanced training in Islamic sciences and Sufism, coupled with his remarkable ability to endure gruelling tests of hardship and self-denial, also won him much praise from his teachers and Sufi masters alike. Although Khwajah Naqshband led a life of denial, sacrifice and single-minded devotion to the practices of Islam, he knew more than anyone else that one cannot attain success in any sphere of human work without a measure of Divine grace, mercy and favour.

Thus, according to Khwajah Naqshband, one cannot choose to be a Sufi for, strictly speaking, a spiritual gift is granted rather than gained, but one should never despair of the mercy and grace of Allah. Like all other great Sufis of the past, he fully understood and accepted this fact. Indeed, Sayyid Amir Kulal, who was one of Khwajah Naqshband's top teachers and spiritual guides, had travelled more than eight miles every week, on foot, to attend religious classes during his training. After twenty years of travelling back and forth, his teacher eventually told him that he had been granted the gift of Islamic spirituality. In the same way, Sayyid Amir Kulal put Khwajah Naqshband through similar sessions of training before confirming that he, too, had been granted the gift of Islamic spirituality.

The Khwajah was a strict follower of Islamic spirituality and self-denial. He would refuse to accept food or gifts offered to him by his local rulers just in case they had been obtained illegally. Once, when he was asked why he refused to keep a servant. He replied, 'Ownership does not go with being a saint.' As a strict follower of traditional Islam, he believed in self-reliance and disliked pleasure-seeking activities. He defined Islamic spirituality as the path of *al-urwa al-wuthqa*, that is, an unbreakable bond between following the Qur'an and the *Sunnah*. In other words, according to the Khwajah, the source of Islamic spirituality was nothing other than the Qur'an and the Prophetic *Sunnah*.

His declaration of the superiority of the Qur'an and the Prophetic traditions over all other sources of guidance was significant and greatly refreshing. This was because, at the time, many misguided Sufis tried to keep aside these two fundamental sources of Islam in their search for the so-called ultimate spiritual experience. Likewise, Khwajah Naqshband was a strict supporter of the Islamic concept of *tawhid* (Divine Unity). He also made a clear distinction between knowledge and understanding of spirituality – as opposed to feeling and experiencing spirituality. He considered the former state to be the peak of tawhid and the latter to be the peak of *ma'rifa* (recognition).

According to the Khwajah's biographers, Abd al-Rahman Jami and Ali ibn Husayn Safi, his spiritual path was first exposed to him in the form of a vision when he was a young man. In that vision, he saw three lamps and a throne. The three lamps represented all the Sufi greats of the past, while the throne was of the great Sufi Abd al-Khaliq Ghujdawani (d. 1179 CE). Khwajah was informed that he had been specially blessed and that he would one day become a great Sufi and an influential promoter of Islamic spirituality and recognition of Allah. The following words of advice were then offered to him in his vision:, 'Whatever happens, always follow the path marked out by divine command and prohibition. Keep a firm resolve and never abandon the Prophetic example and the practice of good works. Keep away from wrong innovations, take the traditions of the blessed Muhammad Mustafa for your guide and make a deep study of all that has been recorded about Allah's messenger and his *sahabah* (companions).'

Although it is not possible to confirm or disprove the truth of this report, there is no doubt that Khwajah Naqshband believed that he was chosen by Allah to seek and spread Islamic spirituality in the light of the Qur'an and the Prophetic *Sunnah*.

Following in the footsteps of his distinguished predecessors such as Abd al-Khaliq Ghujdawani, the Khwajah followed a spiritual path which was in complete harmony with traditional Islam. He avoided the company of those Sufis who became involved in *bida dalala* (heretical or unacceptable innovations). The *naqshbandiyah tariqa* (spiritual order) was initiated by Khwajah Yusuf Hamdani (b. 1048-d. 1140 CE) back in the eleventh century. It then evolved and spread across Central Asia under the leadership of famous Sufis like Abdullah Barqi, al-Andaqi (d. 1157 CE), Yisiwi (b. 1093-d. 1166 CE) and Abd al-Khaliq Ghujdawani before Khwajah Naqshband emerged to become one of its most influential champions.

The mystical philosophy and spiritual method of the early *naqshbandiyah* Sufis was summarised by Abd al-Khaliq Ghujdawani when he said:,

'Learn *fiqh* (Islamic jurisprudence) (*fiqh*) and the *Ahadith* (traditions of the Prophet). Do not mix with illiterate spiritual people ...offer prayers in congregation...do not seek fame... do not accept any office...do not be a security for anybody... do not go to court. Do not mix with rulers or princes...do not construct a *khanqah*... do not hear too much mystic music...

> do not condemn mystic music...eat only what is permitted...
> so far as you can, do not marry a woman who wants mate-
> rial comforts...laughter kills one's heart. Your heart should
> be full of grief, your body as if of an ailing person, your eyes
> wet, your actions sincere, your prayers sincere, your dress
> torn, your company dervishes, your wealth poverty, your
> house the mosque and your friend Allah.'

Although the spiritual practices promoted by Khwajah Yusuf Hamdani and his famous disciples created considerable interest in Islam across Central Asia, the absence of a unified approach to Islamic mysticism prevented ordinary people from harvesting the fruits from the tree of Islamic spirituality. As one of the most prominent Sufis of his generation, Khwajah Naqshband was the most able and qualified person to unify and strengthen the different strands of mysticism which then existed in Central Asia. Although he had extensive knowledge of Islam and was also spiritually very gifted, the Khwajah knew that the task he faced was not an easy one. Thus, after some thinking, he started a mass Islamic spiritual movement which later became known as the *naqshbandiyah* Sufi Order. In doing so, he contributed to the widespread spreading of Islam and Islamic spirituality throughout Muslim Central Asia.

However, unlike, for instance, Jalal al-Din Rumi or Farid al-Din Attar, both of whom were great Sufis and prolific writers, the Khwajah did not write much; rather he became a religious and spiritual reformer *par excellence*. As a devout Muslim, he was horrified to see how Islamic principles and practices were becoming increasingly sidelined in his homeland, if not across all Central Asia. This prompted him to initiate a mass campaign to revive authentic Islamic teachings and practices, and in so doing he hoped to block the forces of materialism and pleasure-seeking in that part of the world.

The movement started by the Khwajah became so popular that over time it became one of the most influential of all Sufi traditions, along with the *qadiriyah tariqa* founded by Abd al-Qadir al-Jilani. Khwajah Naqshband encouraged the followers of his Sufi tradition to spread across Central Asia. They also took its message as far as India where Shaykh Ahmad Sirhindi (see chapter 81), the famous Muslim sage and reformer of India, became one of its leading promoters. The other famous Indian followers of the *naqshbandi-yah tariqa* included Emperor Jahangir (b. 1569-d. 1627 CE), Shah Waliullah of Delhi (see chapter 86) and Sayyid Ahmad Barelvi (b. 1786-d. 1831 CE). In addition to this, Abd al-Rahman Jami, the outstanding Persian writer and poet, was a member of this *tariqa* as were the great Turkish Islamic scholar and reformer 'Bediuzzaman' Sa'id Nursi (see chapter 97) and the Cypriot Sufi Shaykh Muhammad Nazim Adil al-Qubrusi al-Haqqani (b. 1922-d. 2014 CE).

Thanks to the Shaykh Nazim, the *naqshbandiyah* tariqa has today gained thousands of followers in both Europe and America. Likewise, in the Arab world, distinguished scholars like Muhammad Rashid Rida (b. 1865-d. 1935 CE) and Abd al-Ghani al-Nabulusi were connected with this Sufi tradition. In North Africa, Amir Abd al-Qadir al-Jazairi and Sidi Muhammad al-Idrisi were also influenced by the *naqshbandiyah tariqa*. Additionally, Imam Shamyl of Daghestan (see chapter 88), the celebrated Caucasian warrior and freedom fighter, was a member of this Sufi Order. Indeed, when Islam was being brutally suppressed across Central Asia by the Stalinist rulers of the Soviet Empire, it was the followers of this *tariqa* who kept the torch of Islam burning across that region.

Thus, it would not be an exaggeration to say that the Islamic spiritualist movement initiated by Khwajah Naqshband has few parallels in the history of Islam. He breathed his last at the age of seventy-two and was buried in his native village, where a mausoleum was later erected in his memory.

75

Ibn Khaldun
(b.1332 - d.1406 CE) /
(b.733 - d.809 AH)

The Qur'an constantly encourages Muslims to study history and explore the past. In fact, a large portion of the Divine revelation consists of information about the past. The stories of Adam, Nuh, Ibrahim, Musa, Yusuf, Dawud, Mariam and Isa are all related in considerable detail to encourage people to think over and learn lessons from the past. The Qur'anic encouragements inspired the early Muslims to record historical information accurately. Like people of other ancient civilisations, Muslims not only wrote history, but also played a decisive role in the progress and development of history as a subject.

Ancient Greek historians like Herodotus considered history to be only a sequence of events. They did not rigorously examine their data to sift the wheat from the chaff to discover the authenticity of their source material. Nor did they seek to find out the underlying causes of historical events or identify the factors which led to the progress or decline of human society. The root causes of historical progress baffled ancient historians until the Muslims founded historicism (the science of historical inquiry). The father of sociology, the philosophy of history and one of the most influential historians of all time was Ibn Khaldun.

Abd al-Rahman ibn Muhammad ibn Khaldun was born in Tunis, Tunisia into a family of distinguished politicians and civil servants. Of Yemeni origin, Ibn Khaldun's family members settled in Tunis and became prominent figures in Andalusian (modern-day Spain) and North African politics and public affairs. However, his father chose to pursue academic research rather than become a politician. As a noted scholar of Arabic language, literature, Islamic jurisprudence, *Hadith*, Sufism and poetry, he supervised his son's early education at home. He ensured that young Ibn Khaldun learned the whole Qur'an by heart while he was still in his early teens. He then studied Arabic grammar and literature, before pursuing traditional Islamic sciences.

Ibn Khaldun excelled in his studies and completed intensive training in Arabic grammar, theology, and Islamic spirituality and specialised in the *fiqh* of the *Maliki madhhab* (Islamic jurisprudence as interpreted by Malik ibn Anas of Madinah) under the guidance of leading *Maliki* scholars. He combined his studies in *ulum al-din* (Islamic sciences) with thorough training in the *ulum al-aqliyah* (philosophical sciences) including metaphysics, logic, mathematics, philosophy and medicine.

Ibn Khaldun's extensive training in both the Islamic and philosophical sciences not only expanded his intellectual horizon but also powerfully sharpened his mind. He was raised in a politically active family and received a thorough education in the religious and philosophical sciences. That is why he was able to go beyond the superficial and observe things as they were in reality. Since he was a talented student, he liked to question and analyse received wisdom. Indeed, his intellectual questioning and curiosity enabled him to understand and grasp things which others failed to see. Not surprisingly, he became one of the most insightful observers of human behaviour and society in history.

Although Ibn Khaldun continued his formal education until he was about eighteen, his education was frequently interrupted by a combination of natural and man-made disasters and tragedies. On one such occasion, a significant part of the Muslim world was ruined by a deadly plague. This epidemic caused destruction across the Islamic world and almost destroyed the population of Tunis. Ibn Khaldun lost his parents, close relatives and teachers during this dreadful period in the history of North Africa. This left the twenty-year-old Ibn Khaldun rather lonely and isolated. Devastated by his loss, he turned down the offer of a civil service job and went to Fez, in modern-day Morocco, which at the time was one of North Africa's most prosperous cities.

Here he joined the civil service of Sultan Abu Inan, the ruling Marinid monarch, and engaged in advanced training in Islamic and philosophical sciences under the instruction of the city's leading scholars. By combining his studies with government employment, he gained direct access to high-ranking politicians, and civil administrators and also gained first-hand knowledge and experience of political life. His theoretical knowledge of science, mixed with his practical experience of working within the civil service, sharpened his understanding of politics, public affairs and the social relationships in his society.

The faint-hearted rarely succeed in the uncertain world of politics. But Ibn Khaldun was not one of them. He succeeded in his new role as a political administrator. Sultan Abu Inan was so impressed with his performance that he promoted him to a position of considerable political status. He thus became a high-ranking politician who had considerable political power and influence in North African public life. He was still in his early twenties. He continued to serve Sultan Abu Inan conscientiously until he was accused of disloyalty and subsequently imprisoned. After Abu Inan's death, Ibn Khaldun was released by his successor and returned to political life. He was barely twenty-eight when he was appointed a *qadi* (judge) ason he was an expert in *maliki* jurisprudence. However, he found his new job very tiresome and repetitive.

This prompted him to leave North Africa and move to Granada in Spain. He thrived in the existing culture of political uncertainty and social unrest as he was not keen on leading a quiet and lonely life. Not surprisingly, his biography reads more like an action-packed James Bond story than the life of one of history's most influential Muslim thinkers. After he moved to Granada, he received a warm reception from its ruling elites including Ibn al-Khatib, the learned Chief Minister of the State, who later became one of his closest allies. Both were intellectuals and politicians and had many things in common, especially their passion for learning which strengthened their friendship. However, later mutual jealousy and rivalry drove them apart in a hostile way.

Before their falling out, Ibn al-Khatib had nominated Ibn Khaldun to lead a mission to Peter (Spanish: Pedro), the King of Castile. The purpose was to sign a peace treaty between the King and the Muslims of Granada. During this period, Ibn Khaldun visited Seville, the city of his ancestors, and acquired considerable skills and expertise in international politics and diplomacy. On his return to Granada, his reputation as an electrifying speaker, politician and public figure made many of his best friends, including the Chief Minister Ibn al-Khatib, very jealous of him. Thus, they began to make life difficult for him. In the end, he had no choice but to leave Granada and return to North Africa.

At the time North Africa was passing through one of the most unstable periods in its history. Ibn Khaldun found himself caught in the middle of widespread political uncertainty and social disturbance. For the next decade, he led a politically active life, which was often interrupted by periods of personal difficulties and detention. As a result, he suffered, struggled, and faced considerable personal challenges but, on each and every occasion, he came through unharmed. Ibn Khaldun was the ultimate survivor. One day he would be sitting next to the Sultan, while on another day he would find himself locked in a prison. His political life was neither static nor dull; rather he was a risk-taker whose whole life was full of drama, uncertainty and suspense. Everywhere he went, he found himself caught in the middle of political plots, coups and conspiracies.

Tired of political uncertainty, he eventually withdrew from public life for good and began to pursue his intellectual and literary interests. He was around forty-five when he settled with his family in a quiet location and spent the next four years living like a hermit. He then authored his huge and internationally famous text, 'The Book of Instructive Examples and Register of Subjects and Predicates Dealing with the History of the Arabs, Persians and Berbers'. This immortalised him and made him globally famous.

Being a brilliant intellectual, he understood the nature of social trends and the factors which influenced historical change better than anyone else. Thus, he formulated a fresh and innovative method for analysing human culture. He also explained the factors which led to the rise and decline of societies. Ibn Khaldun was not interested in merely explaining the external factors which contributed to social and historical change. He was eager to identify and explain the underlying causes of such happenings. In other words, he was determined to investigate the relationship between the *zahiri* (external) and *batini* (internal) factors which contributed to the rise and decline of cultures and civilisations. Applying his unique scientific approach to understanding human culture and society, he systematically analysed the external data and the internal currents of change, to demonstrate the true nature of social phenomena and historical changes.

According to Ibn Khaldun, a scientific analysis and interpretation of external data showed that there was an underlying rational structure behind all social and historical events. By exploring the nature of social organisation, identifying the nature and characteristics of leadership, and exploring the impact of the environment on human character, personality and social ethos, he was able to demonstrate that a combination of factors – some of which were external, while others were internal – contributed to the rise and decline of human culture, society and civilisation.

Indeed, he analysed the North African Berber society and discovered that the group with the strongest *asabiyah* ('social solidarity') tended to dominate those that lacked a similar sense of social unity and cohesion until there eventually emerged a unified political structure (for example, a monarchy) which expressed their social solidarity. Following further socio-cultural expansion and political consolidation, a new civilisation emerged. This, in turn, led to the formation of urbanised towns and cities where cultural, artistic and scientific pursuits flourished, until the people began to surrender to the lures and temptations of luxuries and pleasure, which caused the age of decline and disintegration.

No other historian or social philosopher, before or after him, had been able to analyse human culture and history in such a thoroughly modern, scientific and innovative manner. In fact, he was the first historian and philosopher to develop an integrated approach to the study and interpretation of human history and culture. And, in so doing, he effectively launched what is today known as 'sociology' or 'social science', even though he referred to it as the 'science of culture'. Not surprisingly, he is today widely considered to be the founding father of both the sociology and philosophy of history.

Ibn Khaldun completed his world-famous book *Muqqadimah fi'l Tarikh* (Introduction to History) at the age of fifty. In the first part, he developed his new theoretical approach to socio-historical analysis of culture, society and civilisation. Sir Arnold J. Toynbee, the celebrated British historian, rated this book so highly that he described it as 'undoubtedly the greatest work of its kind that has ever yet been created by any mind in any time or place.'

In the second part of the book, Ibn Khaldun analysed the history of the Arabs, up to his own time. In the third and last part, he provided a historical account of Western Islam, including the history of the Berbers of North Africa. His autobiography, entitled *al-Ta'rif*, also appears at the end of the third book. This autobiography contains valuable information about his background, childhood, early education and career as a politician and judge.

After completing this monumental book, Ibn Khaldun travelled to Egypt to perform the *hajj* in 1382 CE. He was unable to go to Makkah, and instead, he went to Cairo where he began to deliver regular lectures on political thought, Islamic history and *Maliki* jurisprudence at the world-famous al-Azhar University. His vast knowledge of Islamic law and jurisprudence prompted the Mamluk Sultan al-Zahir Barquq, the reigning monarch of Egypt, to appoint him a judge. But soon he became embroiled in yet another political coup and more conspiracy.

During this period, he suffered a great shock when his wife and seven children perished in a shipwreck en route to Cairo. This prompted him to go to Makkah and perform the *hajj*. At the same time, he also visited Damascus and Palestine, including the historic city of Jerusalem. He then volunteered to go and meet Amir Timur (see chapter 76) to discourage this fearsome Mongol conqueror from attacking Damascus. After his return to Cairo, he spent the next five years of his life in peace and tranquillity.

He died at the age of seventy-four and was buried in the Sufi Cemetery on the outskirts of Cairo. Ibn Khaldun's inspiring personality and vast learning, together with his remarkable contribution to the development of modern social science and philosophy of history, represents an important milestone in the records of human thought. It is very doubtful whether great Western scholars and thinkers (such as Arnold J. Toynbee) would have achieved as much as they did without Ibn Khaldun's seminal contributions to the field of social science and history. That is why humanity will forever remain indebted to this most profound and original Muslim thinker.

76

Timur the Conqueror (b.1336 - d.1405 CE) / (b.737 - d.808 AH)

There is no doubt that Alexander the Great, Genghis Khan, Hannibal and Napoleon were great conquerors. Alexander burst out of Macedonia in 334 BC and overthrew the mighty Persian Empire, although unfavourable circumstances forced him to return home without conquering India. After starting a series of remarkable victories within a short period, he died at the age of around thirty-two.

The Mongols, led by Genghis Khan, suddenly emerged from North-east Asia and rapidly conquered China, India, Persia and southern Russia. The Mongols' reputation for carrying out wholesale massacres and brutality made their opponents shake in their boots. Genghis Khan died in 1227 CE after falling off his horse. Hannibal, on the other hand, was appointed commander of the Carthaginian army when he was only twenty-six. With an army of forty thousand men, thirty-eight elephants and some horses, he fought a brutal battle against the Romans and successfully conquered northern Italy. Fearing betrayal, he poisoned himself in 184 BCE.

By contrast, Napoleon Bonaparte received training at the military academy in Paris and fought numerous battles before becoming the Emperor of Europe. Following crushing defeats at Leipzig

(1814 CE) and Waterloo (1815 CE), he died in 1821 CE. By all accounts, these conquerors were very brave and gifted military leaders who performed wonders on the battlefield, but they all become insignificantce when compared with Timur, who was undoubtedly history's most successful conqueror.

Amir Timur, known as Tamerlane in the West, was born into a noble Muslim family in a village near Shakhrisabz (the Green City) in modern-day Uzbekistan. His father, Taraghay, was the chief of the Barlas tribe. They originally came from the north-eastern region of Mongolia and settled in Central Asia, during the time of Genghis Khan. Historically, the Central Asian region had been a melting pot for people of different racial, cultural and linguistic backgrounds, including nomads from Mongolia, Persians, Turks, Arabs and Europeans. People of all backgrounds gathered in the region. They mixed with the local people and created a lively and distinctive social and cultural environment there.

Since the cold, harsh and treacherous terrain of the steppes made their surroundings very miserable and dangerous, the locals adapted themselves to the unfriendly environment by establishing their own versions of close-knit, nomadic shelters. The name Timur, meaning 'lion', says much about the character, attitude and aspirations of the families of Genghis Khan. These families became known as the Tartars who were tough, resilient and ruthless warrior-like people. They became famous for their bravery, sense of purpose and military prowess. Then again, such qualities and attributes were necessary for leading a successful nomadic life.

Timur was brought up under the careful supervision of his parents and preferred to play games rather than purusue education during his early years. After receiving training in warfare , archery and horse riding, he became a skilled hunter. During this period, he suffered a serious injury which earned him the nickname 'Timur the Lame'. It is originated from the Persian, *Timur-i Lang*. For this reason, he later became known in the West as Tamerlane. Despite his crippling injury, he became an talented polo and chess player. His determination to overcome his disability earned him much respect from his fellow tribesmen. Unlike his pious and religious father, who used to spend much of his time in the company of religious scholars and Sufis, Timur became fascinated by combat and warfare. As expected, he followed the traditions of his people and became a skilled archer, huntsman, soldier and military tactician planner. The art of combat, which he learned during his early years, later helped him when he unleashed his tribal warriors against his enemies across Central Asia, the Middle East and parts of Africa.

Timur was born during a chaotic period in the history of Central Asia. After the death of Genghis Khan, the Mongol Empire began to breakake up rapidly as his descendants engaged in a lengthy succession battle. During the disturbance, the Mongol chiefs created their own territories, thus dividing the Mongol Empire among themselves. Young Timur witnessed the bitter political rivalry which happened at the time between Amir Qazaghan of Mawara' al-Nahr and Tughlugh Timur Khan of Moghulistan. The two men fought tooth and nail for power until Amir Qazaghan was assassinated. This prompted the Tughlugh ruler to start military action against the area known as Mawara' al-Nahr (the land beyond the river or Transoxania) to reunify the two territories under his political leadership. When the news of his march towards Mawara' al-Nahr was relayed to Haji Beg, the chief of the Barlas clan, he chose to flee rather than fight and defend his homeland.

Timur went with Haji Beg and went as far as the Oxus River before he had a sudden change of heart. He returned to Barlas with a group of young fighters and decided to defend his homeland against the invading ruler of Moghulistan. On his return home, however, he decided not to resist the Tughlugh because he felt it would be a pointless task given the size of his army. Instead, he offered his services to the ruler of Moghulistan, who rewarded him handsomely and made him the leader of the Barlas clan. Timur was only twenty-five at the time. Although Timur hated Tughlugh and was eager to force him out of Mawara' al-Nahr, difficult political circumstances forced him to unite with him.

Then again, given his inadequate resources, he could not dare to challenge Tughlugh. So, he decided to establish an partnership with Amir Husayn, the grandson of Qazaghan, who at the time was the ruler of Balkh (located in northern Afghanistan). Timur strengthened his relationship with Amir Husayn by marrying his sisterand also agreed to collaborate with him to overthrow Tughlugh. Things did not work out as they planned and both were forced to go underground. After conducting several years of guerrilla warfare, Husayn fled, leaving Timur to fight on his own. His guerrilla activities eventually ended with the downfall of the small Sarbadar Kingdom of Samarqand. After the overthrow of the Sarbadars, he appointed himself as the new ruler of that kingdom. He then removed Amir Husayn, the ruler of Balkh, from his path and now became the supreme ruler of Chaghatay in Central Asia at the age of thirty-four.

With Chaghatay firmly under his control, Timur focused his attention on the neighbouring States of Qungirat and Moghulistan. Before starting a large-scale military campaign against them, he decided to strengthen his forces with sufficient weaponry and food supplies. He achieved this by transferring Amir Husayn's assets from Balkh and distributing everything amongst his fighters. As a strong, fearless and intelligent warrior, Timur trained and rewarded his fighters better than any of his rivals; likewise, he became well-known for his generosity to his family, friends and guests alike. Unfortunately, his fierce and ruthless behaviour on the battlefield often overshadowed his frequent acts of kindness and generosity.

In truth, Timur was his own man and was motivated more by warfare than anything else, and if anyone dared to cross his path or challenge his authority, he ruthlessly defeated them. His desire to gain victory over his enemies kept him on his toes – even when the odds were firmly stacked against him. As a natural-born fighter, he thrived in the lion's den so much so that on one occasion, when he was locked in a pest infested shed by his enemies, he managed to escape completely unharmed. Being a ruthless and ambitious warrior, he was not interested in ruling a small kingdom; he was determined to conquer and rule the whole world.

After mobilising his forces in 1370 CE, he led an expedition against the Moghul ruler Qamar al-Din but, on this occasion, he only managed to partially beat his rival. He then launched several other military campaigns against the Moghuls before finally defeating them. During this period, he also fought on a northern front, launching attacks against Khwarazm. As a beautiful and fertile territory, Khwarazm was famous for its fruits and agricultural produce and had previously captured the imagination of Ibn Battuta (see chapter 73), the famous Muslim adventurer, when he visited that region during the fourteenth century. After capturing this territory, Timur arranged a regular supply of fresh fruit and vegetables for his forces. He then returned to Samarqand, only to discover his son, Jahangir, had died of flu. Stricken with grief, he could not be consoled. He struggled to come to terms with his loss because Jahangir was his oldest and most beloved son. After a period of mourning, he regained his composure and again plunged himself into the grand theatre of warfare and conquest.

With the areas of Mawara' al-Nahr and Khwarazm now firmly under his control, in 1379 CE he turned his attention towards the Kart dynasty which, at the time, ruled a large territory including most of modern Afghanistan. After consolidating his armed forces, Timur marched into the historic city of Herat without any opposition. He then pushed on towards Mazandaran and captured this territory. The Persian city of Sultaniya was a strategically important centre and it surrendered soon afterwards. This was followed by the takeover of Tabriz, the capital of Azerbaijan. Almost unstoppable, he was now on a rampage.

Thus, in 1387 CE he reached Tbilisi, the capital of Georgia, and raided the entire city. After overpowering Azerbaijan, Georgia and Armenia, his forces marched towards Asia Minor at lightning speed and captured the historic cities of Isfahan and Shiraz. Timur had carved out a huge empire which extended from Samarqand at one end, to Georgia at the other. He was keen to expand his empire further, so he then turned his eyes towards the Islamic East and soon captured Baghdad. Although the brave people of Baghdad put up a heroic resistance, Timur's forces entered the city and created much devastation there. From Baghdad, his forces then proceeded towards the Caucasus, which is the region around the Black Sea and Caspian Sea.

Later, in 1398 CE, Timur marched into India and conquered Delhi, leaving behind only a pile of dust and rubble. He then captured Aleppo and Damascus in 1400 and 1401 CE, respectively, but his greatest victory was yet to come. In 1402 CE, he took on the might of the Ottoman Empire and inflicted a humiliating defeat on the forces of Sultan Bayazid at the Battle of Ankara. The Ottomans were one of the great superpowers of the time, and Timur's victory over them sent shock waves around the world. Indeed, when the news of the Ottoman defeat was relayed across Europe, the people of that Europe openly celebrated and expressed their thanks and gratitude to Timur, because a significant part of Europe at that time was firmly under Ottoman control.

Ironically, it took one emerging Muslim power to inflict defeat on another great Islamic superpower. Although this was certainly not the first time that Muslims had ended up fighting fellow Muslims, there is no doubt that Timur's decisive victory over his Ottoman rivals severely undermined their military power and strength, much to the delight of the Europeans. Thereafter, in 1405 CE, Timur set out for his final military campaign against the Ming Emperor of China, but on his arrival in Otrar (in modern Kazakhstan), he died of fever at the age of sixty-nine or seventy-one. Nonetheless, he had already carved out one of the largest empires in history, extending all the way from Siberia to Smyrna, and from Damascus to Delhi and in so doing, he became one of the most powerful men who ever lived.

Timur was not only a remarkable conqueror, but he was also a gifted political administrator. He organised his army with care and great tactical ability. He also devised and applied a workable political and civil administration across his territories which encouraged travellers and traders to engage in commercial activities. This generated much social and economic development across his vast empire. Having said that, Timur was not an average politician, and nor did he pretend to be one; rather he was a gifted warrior, military commander and an exceptionally successful conqueror who became one of history's greatest imperial rulers. As a military genius, he carefully identified his military targets and pursued them most ruthlessly. He had no time for love, emotion or tears, except only for those who were very close and dear to him. He decorated Samarqand, his imperial capital, with beautiful buildings, elegant gardens, impressive mosques, schools and colleges and also recruited religious scholars to teach and pass on knowledge to the locals.

Towards the end of his life, he liked to sit in the company of religious scholars and Sufis. Since he was a product of many conflicting forces, including his nomadic background, Mongol ancestry, Central Asian heritage and Islamic culture, Timur's character and personality also reflected much tension, confusion and contradiction. He lies buried in the Gur-i Amir Mausoleum Complex in Samarqand, today located in the central Asian country of Uzbekistan.

77

Sultan Muhammad II
(b.1432 - d.1481 CE) / (b.836 - d.886 AH)

The Ottoman Empire (known in Arabic as *al-khilafah al-uthmani-yyah*) was one of the most powerful and lasting dynasties to have emerged in Islamic history. It was founded in 1300 CE by the Turkish chief Uthman Bey. He is also known as Osman or Ottoman. This dynasty rapidly expanded under the governance of Uthman's successors. In all, thirty-six Sultans ruled the Ottoman Empire from 1300 to 1922 CE. At its peak, the Ottoman dynasty stretched from Yemen in the Middle East, as far as Greece, Bulgaria, Romania, Hungary, Albania and the former Yugoslav States of Serbia, Croatia, Bosnia, Macedonia and Kosovo in the West. The rise of the Ottoman Empire, therefore, represented a truly fascinating event not only in the history of Islam but also of Europe because Ottoman contributions in the field of arts, science and architecture were remarkably advanced for their time.

More than five centuries of Ottoman achievements and legacy is today admired by Muslims and Europeans alike. By contrast, modern Turkey only comprises a fraction of its former area. Also, caught between its glorious Islamic past and its future aspirations to be an important part of the European Union, today Turkey finds itself at a crossroads. If modern Turkey is confused about its future direction, then the reign of one of its greatest sons, Sultan Muhammad II, represents the complete opposite, as he represents the Ottoman's greatest triumph over its European opponents.

When Sultan Murad II (b. 1404-d. 1451 CE), the father of Muhammad II, ascended the Ottoman throne, he inherited a strong and united empire which he further consolidated during his reign of three decades. In doing so, he established Ottoman dominance across a significant part of Europe, Asia and the Middle East. Muhammad II was born eight years after his father ascended to power. He was considered far too weak to follow in his father's footsteps and take on the enormous responsibility of ruling a vast empire. He was brought up and educated within the royal palace, and received a privileged upbringing and was surrounded by much wealth and luxury. As part of his royal education, he received tutorials in Arabic, the Qur'an and traditional Islamic sciences from some of the best teachers of the time. Since he was restricted to his father's magnificent royal palace, he had very limited contact with the outside world during his early days. But later he acquired a considerable interest in hunting, military tactics and became fluent in five different languages.

When Sultan Murad's health deteriorated, he encouraged his young son to take on both the political and civil responsibilities of the Ottoman Empire. While he was still in his teens, Muhammad was appointed governor of the province of Amasya by his father to prepare him to ascend the Ottoman throne after his death. Sultan Murad II died and as expected, he was succeeded by his son, who became known as Sultan Muhammad II. He was barely twenty at the time. The young ruler quickly took the challenge of political leadership and started many reforms which were needed within the Ottoman political system. His courage, sound judgement and ability to carry out necessary reforms at a difficult time in the history of the Ottoman Empire reassured everyone that the affairs of the dynasty were indeed in safe hands.

For the next thirty years, the Sultan sat securely on the Ottoman throne. He carved out a unique place for himself in the books of history by becoming one of the Muslim world's most successful military commanders, strategists and statesmen. As a ruler, he pursued his political and military objectives ruthlessly and this made him one of the most successful rulers of the Ottoman Empire. He also championed the cause of tolerance, co-existence and mutual understanding between all of his subjects. Indeed, Sultan Muhammad was fiercely independent-minded, and he rarely asked others for advice or counsel.

Unlike his predecessors, he preferred to lead a private life and even refused to share meals with his Ministers and viziers. Often, he made decisions individually without even consulting his personal secretaries or military advisors. If anyone dared to question him, he taught them a lesson they never forgot. As for his open opponents, he relentlessly pursued them without any mercy or forgiveness. However, it was his rare combination of foresight, great strategic ability, single-minded dedication to his task and this measure of ruthlessness which enabled the Sultan to pursue his objectives with such efficiency and success.

Soon after ascending the Ottoman throne, he initiated fresh diplomatic missions both in the East and the West. He also signed peace treaties with all the rival powers of his time. This move enabled him to focus his full attention on things closer to home. Although his predecessors did attempt to capture the ancient city of Constantinople from its Christian rulers, they failed to breach the city's heavily fortified walls. After the Prophet of Islam prophesied the Muslim conquest of the city back in the seventh century, Muslim armies had been knocking on its doors repeatedly, but without much success. Caliph Mu'awiyah ibn Abi Sufyan (see chapter 10) was one of the first Muslim rulers to send an expedition to capture Constantinople. Abu Ayyub al-Ansari, a distinguished companion of the Prophet, accompanied this expedition and died fighting courageously against the Byzantines. He was buried on the outskirts of Constantinople. Many other attempts were later made by other Muslim rulers to annex Constantinople, but they also failed to capture this historic capital.

As destiny would have it, the duty of taking this last fortress of the Holy Roman Empire fell on the shoulders of Sultan Muhammad II. He was keen to expand his rule into mainland Europe and become the most powerful ruler of his time. Thus, the Sultan was determined to liberate Constantinople. The liberation of this city, he felt, would consolidate his position as the undisputed master of the Muslim world and earn him a unique place in the annals of history. Known to antiquity as Byzantium, Constantinople was named after the Roman Emperor Constantine (b. 272-337 CE). He moved the capital of his empire from Rome to this ancient and strategically situated city on the Bosporus Strait and bridged the continents of Asia and Europe. But the Sultan was not in a hurry to take the city. He decided against launching a hasty attack and, like his illustrious predecessors, be forced to retreat without taking the prize. As a gifted military strategist and inspirational leader, Sultan Muhammad II was convinced that he could capture the city even though he knew it would not be an easy task, especially if the past was anything to go by.

To achieve his objective, he knew he had to devise a meticulous plan and execute it with great care and determination. He began by recruiting military experts and engineers from Hungary and paid them handsomely to design a large number of cannonballs and several delivery systems. The engineers worked round the clock to develop 1.5km eight metre long cannons capable of firing stone balls of up to two-and-a-half feet in diameter. Each weighed up to one hundred and fifty pounds. The idea was to fire stone balls at the city's heavily fortified walls to breach them and allow the Ottoman army to enter the city. As the weapons were being prepared, the Sultan gathered his one hundred and fifty thousand strong army, which included his twelve thousand elite infantrymen known as the Janissaries (derived from the Turkish *yen cheri*, meaning new troops). They were also joined by many religious leaders, scholars and Sufi saints who actively encouraged the Ottoman soldiers to fight courageously.

In 1453 CE, the Sultan marched towards Constantinople with his army and camped close to the city's walls. Although he was only twenty-two at the time, the news of his arrival sent shock waves through Constantinople. In response, the reigning Byzantine Emperor Constantine (b. 1405-d. 1453 CE) ordered the city walls to be strengthened further to withstand the Ottoman assault on the city. But the Sultan was in no rush to take the city, so he patiently waited outside the city walls, biding his time and planning the siege. This prompted the Byzantine forces to order more supplies to sustain them during the siege, as they feared the Islamic army would not depart soon. Suddenly, one of the Sultan's Ministers came to him with the news that a saintly Shaykh had informed him that the fall of Constantinople was now imminent. This prompted the Sultan to lay siege to the city in April 1453 CE.

For the next month, the Ottoman army pounded the walls of Constantinople both from the land and sea. The bombardment caused serious damage to the triple-lined and heavily fortified walls of Constantinople. Now large gaps began to appear in the city's walls, although they were not large enough to enable the Ottoman army to enter the city. With limited supplies and only around eight thousand soldiers, the Byzantine Emperor managed to put up a good fight. But without any external assistance from other European nations, he knew he was fighting a losing battle. Despite his repeated appeals to his fellow Christians across Europe, he received no help or support from any European nations.

If they had responded, it is doubtful whether Sultan Muhammad would have been able to take the city. As it happened, after weeks of heavy bombardment, the Ottoman army failed to make much progress. The defence put up by the Byzantines proved highly effective both on land and on sea. The problem required a swift and cunning solution. The Ottoman ships had been unable to break through the chain boom laid across the mouth of the Golden Horn (the sea inlet protecting the northern side of the city).

It was at this point, with the siege of Constantinople reaching its climax, that the Sultan showed his true colours as a military genius. He ordered his fleet of vessels to be transferred from the Bosporus into the Golden Horn by land. All his generals assured him this was a mission impossible. Typical of the Sultan, he brushed their objections aside and ordered his army to construct a road. This was made from wooden planks, from one end of the Bosporus and leading to the Golden Horn. Animal fat was then applied to grease the planks so that the Ottoman fleet, which consisted of more than eighty large vessels, could 'sail' overland and into the Golden Horn under the cover of darkness.

Arriving within a few hundred yards of the northern walls of Constantinople, the Ottoman army took the enemy by complete surprise. From the sea, the vessels opened fire from the north, while the troops on the ground simultaneously launched cannonballs from the west, and in so doing they smashed the walls of Constantinople to rubble. The Sultan then performed his second miracle and called on his twelve thousand elite infantrymen, the Janissaries and they who attacked and routed the remaining enemy forces. The Ottoman army, led by the Sultan, then marched into the historic city of Constantinople. As for the Byzantine Emperor and his troops, they died fighting bravely, but the victorious Ottomans entered the city greeted by shouts of *Allahu akbar* (Allah is Greater).

By conquering the historic city of Constantinople, the Sultan became known to future generations as *al-fatih*, meaning 'the Conqueror'. After entering the city, he changed its name to *Istanbul* (the city of Islam). Now the more than eight-hundred-year-old prophecy of the Prophet Muhammad, which predicted the fall of Constantinople, became a reality on 29th May 1453 CE. As expected, the Sultan went straight to the splendid surroundings of the Hagia Sophia (Aya Sofia), offered his prayers there and thanked the Almighty for the monumental victory granted to Islam. When a large city like Istanbul is captured after a long battle, normally looting and plundering happen. But the Sultan acted swiftly to ensure no such disorder and lawlessness broke out. He treated the inhabitants of the city with respect and courtesy, allowing the Christians and Jews to continue to live there with their wealth and properties if they so wished.

To reassure his non-Muslim subjects, he even crowned the Greek patriarch with his own hands. Thereafter, he began to rebuild the city's political, civil and educational infrastructure. Unlike the city's previous Byzantine ruler, the Sultan's sense of fairness, justice, equality and tolerance surprised the city's non-Muslim inhabitants. In addition to retaining all the city's historic buildings and institutions, he also refurbished all the buildings which were damaged during the siege. He also ordered two minarets to be added to the exquisite Hagia Sophia, which came to symbolise Islam's great victory over its Byzantine rival. He then transferred the capital of the Ottoman Empire from Adrianople (Edirne) to Constantinople (Istanbul). Most astonishingly, the Sultan was only twenty-two years old when he achieved the unprecedented feat of conquering Constantinople.

During the next twenty-eight years of his reign, he helped to rebuild and repopulate the entire city. In doing so, he transformed Istanbul into one of the world's most beautiful and fascinating cities, thus reflecting its former glory again. As a generous patron of culture and the arts, the Sultan also commissioned the construction of mosques, schools, colleges, and hospitals and promoted art, architecture and education throughout the Ottoman Empire. At the height of his power, the Sultan was considered to be the undisputed leader of the Islamic world. The Ottoman Empire became one of the great superpowers of its time. His large army, consisting of well-paid and professional troops, was feared more than any other military force of the time. And his fleet of vessels, which roamed the seas without any opposition, was also considered to be the world's most advanced naval power of the time.

After capturing Greece and going as far as Italy, the Sultan effectively became the Muslim world's, and also Europe's, most powerful political and military leader. The fall of Constantinople marked the end of the medieval era and started the next phase of the Renaissance and the ages of discovery and colonisation. There is no doubt that his thirty-year reign represented a glorious period in the history of Islam. But it was as the conqueror of Constantinople that he became famous both in the East and the West. The venerable Sultan died at the age of forty-nine. He was the first Muslim ruler to be buried in Istanbul. Thanks also to him, today we still hear people talk about 'the day the ships came sailing overland'.

78

Mimar Sinan
(b.1490 - d.1588 CE) /
(b.895 - d.997 AH)

Muslims not only dominated science, mathematics and philosophy during the medieval period, they also contributed considerably to the development of the arts and architecture. Indeed, some of the world's most beautiful and historic buildings were constructed by the Muslims under the sponsorship of influential rulers like Abd al-Malik ibn Marwan (see chapter 16), Abd al-Rahman III (see chapter 43), Sulayman the Magnificent (see chapter 79) and Emperor Shah Jahan (see chapter 83).

Whether it was the magnificent Alhambra in Granada; the exquisite Sulaymaniyyah Complex in Istanbul; the immortal Taj Mahal in Agra; the incredible Badshahi (Royal) Mosque in Lahore; the revolutionary Sears Tower in Chicago; the breathtaking Dome of the Rock in Jerusalem; the impressive Umayyad Mosque in Damascus; the historic al-Azhar University in Cairo; the elegant Friday Mosque in Isfahan or the remarkable Salimiyah Complex in Edirne, Muslims built these and numerous other impressive buildings and historical monuments throughout the ages, symbolising the beauty and artistic dimension of Islam like never before.

Often, great works of architecture are produced by great architectural minds and the Muslim world has produced some of the world's great architectural geniuses including Muhammad Tahir Agha and Mahmud Agha, the two brothers who built the magnificent Blue Mosque in Istanbul. Fazlur Rahman Khan (b. 1929-d. 1982 CE), was the brains behind the Sears Tower in Chicago, which was once the world's tallest building. But the greatest Muslim architect, and arguably the most creative builder of all time, was Sinan.

Mimar Sinan was born in the central Anatolian province of Kayseri (Qaisariyah) in present-day Turkey. Of Greek origin, his father, Abd al-Mannan, embraced Islam and became a notable member of the Ottoman civil and administrative service. Sinan was therefore born and brought up in a family noted for its services to the Ottomans. Like his father, young Sinan became a loyal supporter of the Ottomans. During his early years, he showed no signs of the great imperial architect that he was to become. After completing his early education, he followed in his father's footsteps and joined the Janissaries – derived from the Turkish *yeni cheri* (meaning 'new troops') – to serve the powerful Ottoman army. It was founded by the Ottomans in the fourteenth century to strengthen their army. The Janissaries were an elite military force, which is what prompted Sinan to join this fearsome and equally admired group.

He must have been physically very strong and well-disciplined because only the very brave and loyal were allowed to join this elite force. The Janissaries were professionally trained soldiers, recruited from across the Ottoman Empire, but especially from the Balkans. The recruits were given Turkish names, offered tutorials in Islam and trained in all aspects of warfare before they graduated with military honours. As the Sultan's elite soldiers, they were also rewarded handsomely for their bravery, unflinching support and superior military skills.

Thanks to his physical skill, sharp intellect and organisational ability, Sinan won instant recognition within the Ottoman army. But it was his contribution as a tactical operator, military strategist and designer of military equipment and devices which earned him an enviable position in the Ottoman army. During the reign of Sultan Salim I (Selim), he helped build more than one hundred and fifty warships to give the Ottomans navy superiority over their rivals. After Sulayman the Magnificent succeeded Salim I in 1520 CE, the Ottomans launched a large-scale military operation against the Hungarians and subdued Belgrade after seven days of intensive bombardment. Sinan and the Janissaries played a vital role in the fall of Belgrade.

Then, Sultan Sulayman led a campaign against the island of Rhodes and again Sinan played an important role in the fight against the fanatical Knights of St. John. During this battle, he devised a formidable artillery system which enabled the Janissaries to outsmart their opponents and capture the island. Impressed with Sinan's clever thinking and innovative military tactics, the Sultan swiftly promoted him to the position of Chief of Staff within the Cannon Operations Department of the Ottoman army. He could think and act quickly in the middle of the battle. He built bridges, fixed damaged roads and constructed war vessels at short notice. This enabled the Janissaries to prepare and launch surprise attacks against their opponents and win battle after battle with ease.

After he polished his architectural skills in the Ottoman army, at the age of around forty-nine, Sinan was promoted by Sultan Sulayman to one of the highest posts within the Ottoman imperial court. He became the Sultan's chief architect and builder. The Sultan already had more than a dozen accomplished architects in his service at the time. However, he was determined to recruit Sinan to design and supervise his major building projects. This period marked the beginning of a new phase in Sinan's life. It also proved to be one of the most productive periods in the history of Islamic art and architecture. Under Sultan Sulaiman's patronage, he constructed some of the Muslim world's most dazzling and inspirational works of architecture. Following the Ottoman conquest of the ancient city of Constantinople under the leadership of Sultan Muhammad II, this historic city was renamed Istanbul (the city of Islam) by its new conqueror.

Thereafter, the Ottomans began to transform the skyline of this ancient city by constructing some of the Muslim world's most breathtaking works of architecture. As one of the oldest buildings in Istanbul, the Hagia Sophia (Aya Sofia) had been neglected by the Byzantines. Originally built by Greek architects for Emperor Justinian (b. 482-d. 565 CE), this historic building was thoroughly repaired and restored to its former glory by the Ottomans. This mammoth task was entrusted to none other than Sinan. He refurbished the entire building and added beautiful new minarets to it to symbolise the Ottoman's victory over their old Byzantine rival. As an unusually industrious architect and builder, Sinan pursued his passion for planning and constructing large architectural projects with great energy and enthusiasm and did so well into his later years.

For more than half a century, he worked full-time for three different Ottoman rulers:, Sulayman I, Salim II and Murad III. During this period, he built scores of magnificent mosques, palaces, mausoleums, libraries, schools and bridges throughout the Ottoman Empire (which at the time extended all the way from the Balkans in Europe to Sana in Yemen). In addition to designing and constructing the mausoleums of Abu Hanifah (in Baghdad) and Jalal al-Din Rumi (in Konya, Turkey), he designed and built the seven-hilled city close to the Bosporus.

But his first major architectural project was the Sehzade Mosque Complex in Istanbul. This building was begun in 1544 CE at the request of Sultan Sulayman. He wished to pay a lasting tribute to his son, Prince Muhammad, who died of smallpox at Manisa at the age of twenty-two. Sinan designed and executed this project along the lines of the old Byzantine cross-dome churches, consisting of a mausoleum, religious school, lodging house and kitchen for the poor. It took four years to complete this building but reportedly he was unhappy with the finished product. He considered it to be the work of an apprentice, although it was a highly decorative and impressive structure. But Sinan set himself very high standards and always tried to surpass the Sultan's expectations.

His second major project was the magnificent Sulaymaniyah Mosque Complex in Istanbul. He started to work on this memorable structure only two years after completing the Sehzade Mosque Complex. This building was supposed to represent an architectural statement of Ottoman power, might and glory, thus surpassing all previous works of Ottoman architecture. Sultan Sulayman personally chose the site of the new building. He wanted this building to grace the skyline of Istanbul in the same way the *Qubbat al-Sakhra* (Dome of the Rock) has been gracing the city of Jerusalem for so many centuries. In 1550 CE, after meticulously preparing for this colossal task, Sinan laid the foundation stone of this building in the presence of the Sultan himself. He was very keen not to let this golden opportunity to build an architectural masterpiece pass by because the Sultan took such a great interest in the project.

According to Mustafa Ali, the famous Ottoman historian, Sultan Sulayman was an outstanding ruler and equally, a prolific builder who was determined to leave his mark in the annals of Islam by constructing some of the Muslim world's most breathtaking works of architecture. The Sultan therefore wanted the Sulaymaniyah Mosque Complex to be one of the world's most impressive and elegant buildings. Sinan worked on this massive project round-the-clock for seven years. He planned and supervised the work from start to finish with great care and precision. Like the Sultan, he was determined to produce an architectural masterpiece which would rise over the great city and reflect the glory of Islam, the Sultan and his empire. In 1557 CE, the Sulaymaniyah Mosque Complex was formally opened by the Sultan and helped to completely transform the skyline of Istanbul for good. After completing this project, Sinan was so pleased with the finished product that he considered it to be one of his best works. But, being a perfectionist, he felt he could do even better in the future.

That opportunity came after Sultan Sulayman died in 1566 CE. Like his father, Sultan Salim II (who was Sulayman's only surviving son) requested the aged Sinan, who was in his mid-seventies at the time, to complete another architectural masterpiece; this one was to be built in Edirne. After meticulously working on the Salimiyah Mosque Complex for nearly a decade, Sinan finally unveiled the building in 1574 CE. After completing this project, he reportedly exclaimed that with Allah's help, he had at last surpassed the Greek architects who had built the ancient Hagia Sophia. The Salimiyah Mosque was the largest of all the Ottoman buildings and is today considered to be one of the world's most beautiful works of architecture. Sinan's creativity, combined with his organisational ability and powerful imagination, enabled him to plan and build some of the most sophisticated and beautiful works of architecture ever executed by a single individual.

His buildings are famous for their elegance, clarity of interior space and simplicity of external design. Indeed, they represented a new and innovative approach to art and architecture. In that sense, Sinan was a unique architect and builder, who understood the need for space, but not at the expense of beauty, elegance and grandeur. All of these elements blended quite remarkably in all his major works. Although the Sulaymaniyah and Salimiyah Mosque

Complexes are today considered to be two of his most impressive works, he actually planned, supervised and built more than three hundred and fifty construction projects in total. These included eighty-one mosques, fifty-five schools, thirty-four palaces, eight bridges and nineteen mausoleums.

Sinan was not only an industrious builder and gifted architect, but he was also a loyal Muslim who served the Ottomans with unsurpassed distinction. He died at the advanced age of ninety-eight and was buried in a mausoleum he had built close to the Sulaymaniyah Mosque Complex in Istanbul. The beauty and elegance of his architectural contribution and legacy will no doubt continue to grace the Muslim world for a long time to come. Indeed, his achievements are second to none in the annals of Islamic art and architecture.

79

Sulayman the Magnificent (b.1494 - d.1566 CE) / (b.900 - d.974 AH)

Historians often classify Islamic history into what is known as the 'classical' and 'modern' periods. Two of the greatest empires of the classical period were the Umayyad and the Abbasid dynasties which collectively ruled the Muslim world for around six centuries without serious opposition. But this was not the case during the modern period. The political situation shifted radically within the Muslim world following the emergence of several regional powers. Three of the most influential political powers of this modern period were the Ottomans (fl. 1300-1922 CE), the Safavids (f. 1501-1722 CE) and the Mughals (fl. 1526-1857 CE).

Like the Safavid and Mughal dynasties, the Ottomans left a remarkable and long-lasting historical and cultural legacy. At the height of its power, the Ottoman Empire extended across three continents, namely Europe, Africa and Asia. It was founded in 1300 CE by Uthman Bey (b. 1258-d. 1326 CE), a Turkish chief. The Ottoman Empire became an awesome political and military superpower during the sixteenth century under the wise and able leadership of Sulayman the Magnificent, the tenth ruler of the Ottoman Empire.

Sulayman was born in the Asiatic province of Trabzon. His great-grandfather was Sultan Muhammad II, the conqueror of

Constantinople (see chapter 77). His father, Sultan Selim I, ascended the throne late in life in 1512 CE and ruled for eight years with some success. His mother, Aishah, was a noble lady who became his first tutor and guide. Known to have been very wise and handsome, Sulayman grew up under the watchful gaze of his loving parents. As the Sultan's only son, he was groomed for political and military leadership from the beginning. Thus, he was expected to lead the vast Ottoman Empire into the new century. His early education consisted of tutorials in Arabic, the Qur'an and Islamic legal, ethical and moral principles and practices. Later he gained first-hand knowledge of political and civil administration as governor of Crimea and other provinces. This provided him with much-needed experience in political administration and diplomacy before he sat on the Ottoman throne.

In 1520 CE, Sultan Selim died at the age of fifty-four. He had successfully led a series of military attacks and strengthened Ottoman rule across much of Europe, Asia and Africa. As expected, Sulayman succeeded his father without facing any political or military opposition. He was only twenty-six at the time and instantly became one of the most powerful rulers of his time. The period of Sulayman was unique in history because several other famous rulers such as Emperor Charles V of Germany (b. 1500-d. 1558 CE), Henry VIII (b. 1491-d. 1547 CE) and Queen Elizabeth of England (b. 1533-d. 1603 CE), Francis I of France (b. 1494-d. 1547 CE), Emperor Akbar of Mughal India (b. 1542-d. 1605 CE) and Shah Isma'il of Safavid Persia (b. 1487-d. 1524 CE) became witnesses to each other's greatness.

However, Sulayman outshone all his contemporaries by the force of his magnificent character and personality. As the ruler of the vast Ottoman Empire, which extended all the way from Europe as far as the Middle East and Asia, he filled the length and breadth of his dominion with peace, justice, fairness, tolerance and prosperity. With Islam being the official religion of the State, Sulayman made Turkish the main language of his empire and promoted it throughout his dominion.

As a gesture of goodwill, immediately after ascending the Ottoman throne, he abolished all the harsh policies which were applied by his father during his reign. He also freed all the slave labourers his father had brought from Egypt. He restored all the money, goods and properties confiscated by his father from the Ottoman traders for engaging in trade with the Safavids, who were their main rivals. Sulayman's wise and decisive actions instantly won over the people to his side. He made it clear that he would not tolerate injustice and oppression, no matter who happened to be the perpetrator. He then took action to root out bribery and corruption from within the Ottoman central government, as well as provincial political and administrative circles. His wide-ranging reforms, combined with his determination to eradicate political corruption from within the Ottoman government, made him very popular with his people who soon became very fond of him for his wisdom, generosity and fair play.

Since the main purpose of his reforms was to eradicate injustice and corruption from all levels of his administration, he established an imperial council (divan). This consisted of government Ministers, senior civil servants, military generals, regional governors, senior judges and some of the most prominent *ulama* (religious scholars) of the time. The members of this council were required to oversee the affairs of the State and regularly discuss and debate all the significant issues of the day. They were also required to monitor existing governmental policies and, where appropriate, produce new policy proposals, although the final decision always rested with the Sultan himself. By restructuring and reorganising the Ottoman government, Sulayman hoped to communicate and engage directly with his subjects. This also enabled his people to voice their concerns and provide regular feedback on the performance of his government.

After setting up the imperial council, Sulayman reformed the outdated Ottoman legal system. He was not interested in fixing parts of the system; rather he completely overhauled the entire legal system to ensure that justice, fairness and equality prevailed across his empire. The legal system implemented by Sulayman enabled both Muslims and non-Muslims to seek redress for their grievances through the Ottoman courts. These courts applied a combination of *Sharia* (Islamic law) and imperial *Qanun* (Ottoman law).

Like the other Ottoman rulers, Sulayman's political thinking was influenced by his desire to see peace, justice and prosperity exist across his dominion. Indeed, their desire to render justice and win the hearts and minds of their people often provided the Ottoman rulers with much-needed political legitimacy. For this reason, Sulayman was determined, if not ruthless, in his pursuit of political, legal and administrative reforms. It was not long before he succeeded in restoring peace, security and prosperity across the Ottoman Empire, thus further consolidating his position as the supreme ruler of the Muslim world. Impressed by his political, social, economic and legal reforms, his subjects conferred on him the popular title of the *qanuni* (or 'law-giver).

With peace and prosperity restored throughout the Ottoman Empire, Sulayman turned his attention to international politics and diplomacy. At the time, the rebellious activities of the governor of Syria became a pressing issue for him. He may have been a gentle, peace-loving and generous sovereign, but he was far from being anti-war. Faced with open rebellion in Syria, he assembled a large army and sent an expedition to Syria to bring its treacherous governor to heel. In the battle, the governor and his supporters were defeated by Sulayman's forces.

After dispatching a new governor to Syria to oversee the administrative affairs of the country, Sulayman was also forced to act against the King of Hungary for humiliating his representative, who had gone there to collect the annual tax from the King. So it was that in 1521 CE, at the age of twenty- seven, Sulayman organised a large expedition and marched towards the city of Belgrade, which he captured after seven days of heavy fighting. The conquest of Belgrade was a major achievement considering that the city had resisted the Ottomans on more than one occasion, including during the reign of his great-grandfather Sultan Muhammad (Fatih) II. After establishing a military base in Belgrade, he began to devise his next military plan.

A year later, Sulayman moved towards the strategically important Mediterranean island of Rhodes, which was firmly in the grip of the fanatical Knights of St John. When the Knights began to intensify their rebellious activities against the Ottomans, Sulayman decided to deal with them once and for all. Accompanied by a one hundred thousand-strong force and three hundred formidable vessels, he spearheaded a massive military assault on the island. The Knights fought back with great determination and resisted the Ottoman army for nearly nine months before they were forced to surrender. But the Sultan treated the people of the island with kindness, sympathy and respect. He also agreed to let those Knights who did not wish to live there anymore leave with their personal belongings.

Then, in 1526 CE, Sulayman authorised one of the most important campaigns of his reign, namely the Ottoman invasion of Hungary. The Ottoman forces were equipped with superior weaponry. They left their military base in Belgrade and marched towards Budapest, the capital of Hungary. In the battle, Louis II, the King of Hungary, and his senior officials died fighting. After building a large military base in Budapest, Sulayman returned to Istanbul, having defeated most of his enemies. But a few years later, Sulayman was again forced to return to Budapest to put an end to a civil war which had broken out there between his governor, Zapolye, and a rival militia led by Ferdinand, the brother of King Charles V of Germany. Following a fierce battle, he entered Budapest and restored peace and security throughout the city.

He then proceeded to Vienna and laid siege to that historic city. This siege lasted nearly three months before a combination of limited provisions, decreasing military supplies and adverse weather forced him to lift the military campaign and return to Istanbul. The Ottoman failure to take Vienna represented a major turning point in both Islamic and European history because this brought an end to the Ottoman advance into the rest of Europe.

As soon as Sulayman lifted his siege on the city, the people of Vienna, and the rest of Europe, rejoiced and celebrated. This day became known throughout Europe as 'the Day of Deliverance'. Subsequently, Sulayman spearheaded many other minor military campaigns across Europe, Persia and Egypt during his reign. History shows he was a veteran military commander who personally led no fewer than thirteen major military expeditions during his rule. Ten of which were in Europe and the other three in Asia. He developed and strengthened Ottoman military power and supremacy like never before. His fleet of warships became one of the world's largest naval powers under the stewardship of his gifted Admiral Khair al-Din Barbarossa so that the Ottoman navy had complete supremacy of the seas. His vast army was also one of the most disciplined and professional combat forces of the time. In short, under Sulayman's able leadership, the Ottoman Empire became one of the world's great military superpowers.

Away from the battlefield, Sulayman distinguished himself as a generous supporter of learning, culture, art, architecture and science. During his reign, he built scores of beautiful and spectacular mosques, schools, colleges, palaces and other similar buildings. His most famous architectural works include the magnificent Sulaymaniyyah Complex built in Istanbul by Mimar Sinan (see chapter 78). Sinan was his personal builder and one of the world's greatest architects. This huge, but equally superb, mosque was meant to symbolise the glory of Ottoman power and might in the form of architecture. Since this period represented the height of Ottoman political, military and architectural achievement, Sulayman also became recognised as the unchallenged ruler and champion of the Muslim world at the time. In addition to the Sulaymaniyyah Complex, he constructed many other impressive buildings including the elegant Salimiyah Complex, the impressive Bayazid Jami mosque and the awe-inspiring Sehzade Complex. These magnificent buildings completely transformed the skyline of the historic city of Istanbul.

As a deeply cultured and enlightened sultan, and an accomplished poet and devout Muslim, Sulayman showered his subjects with money, wealth and gifts at a time when his European counterparts were busy oppressing, looting and humiliating their people. According to the historians of the time, the European visitors to Istanbul returned to their native countries to relate stories about Sulayman's sense of justice, fair play, tolerance and civility. Indeed, the Europeans considered him to be an ideal ruler and rated his achievements very highly. They wished their own rulers were as just, civilised and enlightened as he was. That is why Sulayman became known throughout Europe as *el Magnifico* (the Magnificent). Moreover, he was the first Muslim ruler to develop formal diplomatic relations with several prominent European powers including France, Venice and England, and in so doing he actively promoted trade and commerce with the rest of Europe.

On a personal level, Sulayman was an educated, gentle and determined individual. Being deeply religious, in his spare time he used to commit the Qur'an to paper, and copies of the Qur'an written by his own hand are still in existence to this day. More importantly, he was a humble sultan who ruled his people with understanding, a sense of justice and tolerance. He was not only 'the magnificent'; he was also the greatest of all Ottoman Sultans and arguably one of the Muslim world's most successful rulers. He died at the age of seventy-two and was buried in his beloved Istanbul. After his death, the Ottoman Empire began to decline for all time.

As a civic and political administrator, Nizam al-Mulk proved remarkably efficient and effective. His sharp intellect, coupled with his superior education and diplomatic skills, set him apart from his peers. Being honest, loyal and cultured, Prince Alp Arsalan was also impressed with Nizam al-Mulk's polished administrative and organisational skills. After being swiftly promoted to one of the highest posts within the prince's provincial government, Nizam al-Mulk also proved to be a gifted political operator. Following the death of Tughrul Beg, a lengthy power struggle broke out within the Seljuk royal family. Alp Arsalan eventually emerged victorious and became the Sultan of the Seljuk dynasty. Immediately after ascending the throne, he promoted Nizam al-Mulk to the post of *wazir-i-a'zam* (Prime Minister) of his vast kingdom.

As Prime Minister and one of the Muslim world's most powerful men at the time, he activated a thorough reform of Seljuk's political, economic, social and educational policies. Being Turks, the Seljuks preferred to employ and promote fellow Turks to the highest posts within the Seljuk civil, administrative and military services. But, keen to promote peace and prosperity at home and maintain a powerful army to defend his kingdom from his external enemies, Alp Arsalan broke away from his family tradition. He appointed Nizam al-Mulk, who was of Persian origin, to the highest post in the land. As committed Sunni Muslims, both Alp Arsalan and Nizam al-Mulk became champions of Islamic orthodoxy. They wanted to protect and preserve the Baghdad-based Abbasid Caliphate from the Fatimids of Egypt, who were Shi'a and were planning its downfall. Motivated by their common interests, the Sultan and his Prime Minister worked closely to maintain Seljuk power and continue their domination of the Muslim world.

After becoming Prime Minister of the Seljuk kingdom, Nizam al-Mulk decided to fulfil the promise he made to Umar Khayyam and Hasan-i-Sabbah back in Nishapur during his student days. Accordingly, he called Umar Khayyam to his office in Isfahan and offered him the post of Chief Government astronomer. Khayyam afterwards played a crucial role in the development of a refined calendar (known as the *jalali* calendar). Next, he contacted Hasan-i-Sabbah and offered him a high-ranking post within the Seljuk civil service, but he had become involved in a political conspiracy and was forced to flee to Fatimid Egypt. There he transformed a disgruntled group of Nizari Shi'as into a dangerous political and religious sect.

Known as the Assassins, this group started destabilizing activities against the Seljuks. But, being the Prime Minister of the Seljuk kingdom, Nizam al-Mulk was able to counter their activities very successfully. Indeed, during Alp Arsalan's rule of nine years, he was the sole playmaker in the Seljuk kingdom, while Sultan Alp played only a ceremonial role. This gave Nizam al-Mulk all the freedom he needed to reform the civil and administrative structures of the kingdom. By reorganising and unifying the civil and administrative systems of the government – whose rule extended from Syria to Iran – he was able to stamp out corruption and malpractice and improve accountability and efficiency. Under Nizam al-Mulk's stewardship, the Seljuk dynasty became one of the most powerful, prosperous and culturally advanced dynasties of its time. Being also a wise and educated politician, he promoted learning and education across the vast empire. So much so that he turned it into a thriving centre of commercial activity and Islamic learning, scholarship, culture and arts.

He despised illiteracy so much that he promoted free education throughout the dominion and encouraged the people to pursue higher education, undertake research and expand their intellectual horizons. To facilitate this task, he embarked on one of the most ambitious educational programmes ever undertaken by a Muslim leader. He authorised the construction of a series of large educational institutions throughout the land. Begun in 1066 CE, when he was only forty-six, these educational institutions were established in all the major cities of the Seljuk kingdom including Nishapur, Baghdad and Damascus. They not only became some of the first colleges of their time but also became some of Islamic history's finest institutions of higher education. After constructing the colleges, Nizam al-Mulk went out of his way to recruit some of the brightest minds of the Muslim world to come and teach there. After the college in Nishapur was completed, he hired *imam al-haramayn al-Juwayni* to come and teach there.

Al-Ghazali, who later became one of the Muslim world's most celebrated scholars, also served as Professor of Islamic Thought at the same institution. They were known as *Madrasah al-Nizami-yah* (the Nizamiyah College). These institutions of higher educa-tion were the Harvard and Oxford of their time. Not surprisingly, they produced some of the most famous and legendary thinkers of the Muslim world including Shaykh Sa'di of Shiraz who studied at Nizamiyah College's Baghdad campus. Nizam al-Mulk's spend-ing on education was more than generous. Indeed, he allocated the lion's share of his annual budget to the promotion of learning and education. He was also known for his careful management of Seljuk's finances. But he was exceedingly generous when it came to spending on education.

If Nizam al-Mulk was a great educationalist, then he was an equally successful politician. Being a caring, sensitive and compas-sionate administrator, he took measures to address his people's daily needs and requirements. He not only increased annual food production, but he also introduced a fair tax system. He reformed the *bait al-mal* (public treasury) to improve its efficiency. He close-ly supervised the collection and distribution of *zakat* (obligatory alms). He modernised the roads and reorganised the Seljuk judi-cial system. In addition, he constructed medical clinics and hospi-tals which offered free healthcare and medication to the people. Moreover, he built sufficient mosques to meet the people's spiritu-al needs and stepped up security throughout the Seljuk kingdom to counter crime and banditry.

Following in the footsteps of the Abbasid Caliph Harun al-Rashid (see chapter 28), he built resting places along the main trade routes to encourage and facilitate trade and commerce. He instructed the locals to dig wells to provide free, fresh water to the travellers and merchants alike. In addition, Nizam al-Mulk maintained a well-equipped and disciplined army to defend the Seljuk kingdom from its external enemies. He made it an obligation on himself to go out and personally survey the condition of the people, their towns and cities regularly. He liked to speak to them about their prob-lems, difficulties and hardships. His exemplary conduct won him tremendous respect and affection throughout the vast empire. He also became one of the most influential and revered Muslim states-men of all time – along with Umar ibn Abd al-Aziz (see chapter 19), Abd al-Rahman III (see chapter 43), Sultan Nur al-Din Zangi (see chapter 59), Salah al-Din ibn Ayyub (see chapter 61) and Sulayman the Magnificent (see chapter 79).

Nizam al-Mulk was fifty-two when Sultan Alp Arsalan was brutally murdered. Malik Shah, his son and successor, asked Nizam to stay on as Prime Minister. As it happens, Malik Shah rated him so highly that he crowned him *atabeg* (the father figure). As a wise and skilled political operator, Nizam al-Mulk continued to strengthen the State's security services, which enabled him to defend against the rebellious activities of his enemies with tremendous success. As an adherent of *Shafi'i madhhab* (school of law), he was always in the habit of consulting the outstanding religious scholars of his time (including al-Ghazali) to secure their support for his political and educational programmes.

During his long tenure as Prime Minister, Nizam al-Mulk worked tirelessly to protect and preserve the life, property and dignity of the people. His honesty, integrity and transparency in his dealings with his officials helped to create a just and equitable system of government, one where corruption and malpractice were not tolerated.

After he retired from politics, he wrote a book on political administration for the benefit of young Sultan Malik Shah. It was entitled *Siyasat Namah* (A Treatise on Politics). This book covered all aspects of Islamic political administration, including the role of the Prime Minister and the responsibilities of other government Ministers. It also explained the purpose of the judiciary and the qualities and qualifications required of judges and civil administrators. It discussed taxation policy, state security and espionage, and even how to tackle corruption and rebellion. He wrote this political thought and administrative ideas around three hundred years ago. Undoubtedly, Nizam al-Mulk was one of the Muslim world's most influential educationalists, political thinkers and statesmen. He was attacked by an agent of Hasan-i-Sabbah while he was on his way to Baghdad. He died at the age of seventy-two.

80

Akbar the Great
(b. 1542 - d.1605 CE) /
(b.949 - d.1014 AH)

After the death of Amir Timur in 1405 CE, the vast empire he had created began to rapidly collapse, due to his close descendants fighting each other for overall political control. In the process, they only succeeded in dividing the Timurid Empire into several territories. The fighting forced many of his descendants to flee from Samarqand and seek refuge elsewhere. Zahir al-Din Muhammad (b. 1483-d. 1530 CE), better known as Babar (Babur), was one of them. He descended from two great Asian conquerors. Timur on his father's side and Genghis Khan on his mother's side. Babar marched into Kabul in 1504 CE at the age of twenty-two and established his political base there.

From Kabul, he launched raids into India and overcame his opponents with great skill and determination before establishing Mughal supremacy. Babar, the founder of the Mughal Empire, died soon afterwards without fully strengthening his new kingdom. Humayun, his son and successor, was too romantic, fun-loving and indecisive to make much of an impact. He also died in his forties without securing Mughal rule. It was left to the genius of Akbar, the greatest of Mughal Emperors and one of the most influential rulers of Muslim India, to fully consolidate Mughal rule throughout the subcontinent.

Jalal al-Din Muhammad was born in Umarkot in the northern Indian province of Sind (in present-day Pakistan). His father, Humayun (b. 1508-d. 1556 CE), married Hamida Banu Begum, the daughter of a noble Persian scholar. Akbar was born at a time when his father had lost much of his power to his opponents – including his own brothers – before he took military action to regain his lost territories. Since Humayun had few supporters in Sind, he proceeded to Persia to ask the reigning Safavid monarch, Shah Tahmasp for his political and military support.

Backed by the Safavids, Humayun directed military action against his rebellious brothers Kamran, Askari and Hindal. After defeating them, he acted against the rebellious governors of Lahore, Punjab, Delhi and Agra, and in so doing reasserted his political authority across that region. During this period of military campaigns, Humayun and his family were forced to move from one place to another, which deprived young Akbar of much formal education and training. For this reason, he failed to gain expertise in literacy.

Although harsh political circumstances prevented Akbar from learning to read and write during his early years, later in life he surrounded himself with people who were highly educated. If he wished, he could have acquired literacy skills, but it appears he was not interested, perhaps because he preferred to learn through the spoken word rather than rely on pen and paper. He was blessed with an exceptional memory and sharp intellect. He learned and mastered a wide range of subjects including history, philosophy, religion, art and poetry with ease. During his early years, Akbar's mentor and guide was Bairam Khan, a loyal, trusted and experienced Mughal civil servant, who trained him in all aspects of political, civil and military affairs. He prepared Akbar to succeed his father as the ruler of the Mughal dynasty.

During this period, young Akbar lived with his mother in Punjab. He was a bright, cultured and sensible young man who understood the special position he occupied. He may not have fully understood and appreciated the tremendous responsibility he was expected to shoulder after the death of his father, but Bairam Khan ensured he was prepared for it. Akbar was only thirteen when his father suddenly died in 1556 CE and, as expected, he succeeded him as the ruler of the Mughal Empire. His succession to power was to mark the beginning of a glorious era in the history of Muslim India.

Akbar may have been illiterate, but he was certainly not short-sighted or unintelligent. He knew that his father had tried his best to reassert his authority across the Mughal territories but had failed to achieve all his objectives. After ascending the Mughal throne, he initiated military action to regain the lost territories, and thereby restore political stability, social peace and security across the Mughal dominion. Operating under the guidance and steward-ship of Bairam Khan, he acted against all the remaining rebellious governors and Sultans. He won a decisive victory at Panipat, where he inflicted a crushing defeat on Hemu, his most powerful Hindu rival, who at the time ruled both Delhi and Agra. Although Hemu had assembled a large army, Akbar did not feel intimidated; instead, he bravely marched onto the battlefield with his army and defeated his opponent's forces. This decisive victory strengthened Akbar's position both politically and militarily and enabled him to focus his attention on the north.

Bairam Khan, his chief political advisor and military command-er, had played a decisive role in consolidating Mughal power and authority throughout northern India. However, as Akbar began to tighten his grip on India, the aged Bairam Khan increasingly be-came a liability rather than an asset to the Mughals, due to his political authoritarianism and heavy-handed military tactics. Akbar lost patience with his mentor and guide and dismissed him from his post as chief advisor. He then assumed full political and military responsibility himself. A year later, Bairam Khan was attacked and killed by a dissatisfied Afghan warlord while he was on his way to Makkah to perform the sacred pilgrimage.

Akbar was only eighteen when he became a fully-fledged Mughal ruler and military commander. His bold and decisive action against his political opponents enabled him to strengthen Mughal rule across a large part of India and thereby completely trans-formed the fortunes of his dynasty. He was keen to expand Mughal rule further, so he took the fight to the neighbouring territories. Thus, he conducted military expeditions against the Rajputs of Rajasthan as they began to threaten Mughal interests. He headed a large force and went to attack the Rajputs who were eventually de-feated, despite stiff resistance, due to his superior military power.

After occupying Rajasthan, he proceeded towards the State of Gujarat. With its thriving ports and coastal resorts, Gujarat was a strategically important province and major commercial centre at the time. For this reason, Akbar was very keen to capture this province. Indeed, as soon as he received news of riots in Ahmedabad, the provincial capital of Gujarat, he immediately set off with his forces. He travelled at lightning speed and covered around six hundred miles in just over a week. He took the rebels inside the city completely by surprise. He captured the capital of Gujarat without encountering much resistance and thus connected his empire to the Arabian Sea, thereby opening a naval route to the rest of the world.

Akbar then marched into Surat in 1573 CE. Then Bengal, the wealthy northern Indian province also fell to the Mughals, as did Kabul. A year later, he captured the beautiful valley of Kashmir, and this was followed by Orissa. Sind and Baluchistan also became integral parts of the Mughal Empire. Following this astonishing series of conquests, Akbar managed to establish Mughal power and authority throughout northern India. This period therefore represented the height of Mughal political power and military might. Despite his lack of formal education and training, Akbar was an accomplished ruler and gifted military strategist. Known to have been physically very strong, extremely brave and intelligent, he proved a success both on and off the battlefield.

According to his son Salim (who later became Emperor Jahangir), 'Although he was illiterate, so much became clear to him through constant interaction with the learned and the wise in his conversations with them that no one knew him to be illiterate. He was so well acquainted with the beauty of verse and prose composition that his deficiency was not mentioned. He passed his nights awake and slept little in the day. He counted his wakefulness at night as so much added to his life. His courage and boldness were such that he could mount raging, rutting elephants and subdue them to obedience murderous elephants.'

As an intelligent ruler, Akbar knew that brute force only breaks; it does not mend and fix. Having expanded Mughal rule across such a large area through military force, he knew it would not be possible to unify and strengthen these territories without developing and implementing an effective political and civil administrative system to govern them. Since all the previous Indian Muslim dynasties had disintegrated within a few decades of their establishment, Akbar was determined not to allow the same to happen to the Mughals. But to achieve his objectives, he knew he had to make plans for the long term, establish proper political governance and increase economic growth.

However, he could not achieve this without the cooperation of the public. So, Akbar decided to win the hearts and minds of his people – that is, particularly the Muslims and Hindus – by promoting dialogue and mutual understanding between two of India's most prominent religions. By championing religious dialogue and cultural understanding between Muslims and Hindus, he hoped to establish lasting political stability, social solidarity and cultural understanding and tolerance throughout Mughal India. To achieve this objective, Akbar reformed the existing Mughal political and administrative structure which depended heavily on the goodwill and support of the wealthy, independent feudal chiefs to function effectively. So long as these chiefs remained loyal to the Mughals, they were – in the past – left to their own devices, but this had often led to political mismanagement, economic corruption and social discontent in many parts of India.

Akbar changed this system and instead appointed provincial governors who were responsible for overseeing the affairs of their own provinces and regularly reported directly to him. He then forged alliances with several influential Hindu groups, including the Rajputs, who subsequently joined the Mughal political, civil and military services. In so doing, he ensured that both Muslims and Hindus played an active part within his administration. This strategy proved very effective, not least because Muslims and Hindus came together and helped to consolidate Mughal political power and authority across India. Thus, politically speaking, Akbar's efforts to unite Muslims and Hindus proved a success, but the same cannot be said of his attempts to harmonise Islam and Hindu religion.

As a fiercely monotheistic religion, Islam preaches *tawhid* (the absolute oneness of Allah), thus negating all forms of *shirk* (association). By contrast, Hindus believe in multiple gods and goddesses and also pray to statues, idols and various animals. As such, these two religions are more diametrically opposed to each other than probably any of the other major world faiths. Yet, inspired by his

Timurid ancestry, early contact with Sufism and subsequent encounter with Hinduism, Akbar decided to engage in highly questionable religious and cultural experimentation. Although his motive (namely to develop cultural understanding and religious tolerance between his Muslim and Hindu subjects) was indeed a praiseworthy one, his method of inter-faith dialogue proved both incompetent and foolish. Akbar and his advisors were frustrated by continuous Hindu-Muslim communal rivalry and conflict. They began to explore ways in which they could end these bitter conflicts by emphasising the common elements between the two faiths, rather than focusing on the differences. This eventually inspired them to create a new religious mixture by combining aspects of Islamic spirituality and Hindu philosophy. But, far from uniting the two rival religious factions, this only served to make matters worse, because both orthodox Muslims and Hindus considered Akbar's religious merging very offensive.

Although he was a Muslim, he was now branded a heretic by orthodox Muslims and Hindus alike. The charge of heresy levelled against Akbar was justified, but he was not an unbeliever as such. Indeed, one of his favourite sayings was, 'If I have knowingly taken a step which is displeasing to Allah or have knowingly made an aspiration which was not according to His pleasure, may that elephant finish us, for we cannot support the burden of life under Allah's displeasure.' As a religious freethinker, he was fascinated by religion and philosophy. He regularly engaged in religious discussion and debate with the leading Muslim, Hindu and Christian scholars of his time, for he was very keen to discover the truth about religion.

He accepted the authority of the Qur'an but also believed in the spiritual unity of religions. That is to say, he believed that all religions were true and authentic in their essence; only their forms differed. This became the basis of his new religious mixture, namely *din-i-ilahi* (the Divine Religion). As expected, it was vigorously opposed by both orthodox Muslims and Hindus. Akbar's controversial and highly questionable religious and cultural reforms aside, his long reign of forty-nine years represented one of the most important periods in the history of Mughal India. He established political stability, reformed the Mughal civil administration and promoted economic prosperity across the land. He also built some of India's most magnificent buildings including the breath-taking Fatehpur

Sikri, which is today considered to be one of the most beautiful sites in India.

As a ruler, Akbar was determined and ruthless, but also benevolent. His most famous motto was 'Servant of all and master of none.' Despite being illiterate, he was very fond of books and loved classical Persian poetry, which he regularly had read out to him by his close friends and advisors, Abul Faid and Abul Fadl. Under his able stewardship, the Mughal Empire became one of the most influential political and military powers of the time. He died at the age of sixty-three and was buried inside the mausoleum he had prepared for himself at Sikandra, located about five miles west of Agra, India.

Glossary

Imran Mogra

Al-Mohads – correctly this is *al-Muwahiddun*, from *Wahid* meaning One. Literally those who believe in the oneness of Allah. They were a North African Muslim dynasty (1121 to 1296 CE).

Al-Moravids – correctly this is *al-Murabitun*, from *ribat* meaning a religious fortress. A dynasty which controlled Morocco and its near areas (1076 to 1147 CE). A marabout is a holy person.

Asabiyah – tribal, clan or group solidarity, sometimes used for nationalism.

Asceticism – see *zuhd*.

Austere – living with no luxuries, strict in manners, having a plain appearance. See *Zuhd*.

Bait al-hikmah – House of Wisdom, an Academy founded in 830 CE by Caliph Harun al-Rashid in Baghdad for the purpose of research, translation, teaching and learning.

Batini – hidden, any doctrine which is inner and secretive. It also refers to someone who belongs to a group with such beliefs. It also refers to doubtful doctrines.

Black Death – a deadly epidemic plague which killed millions in the mid-1300s.

Byzantine – The Byzantine Empire was a vast and powerful civilisation. It existed from 330 until it fell in 1453 CE to the Ottoman army who defeated Constantinople. It is often called the Eastern Roman Empire or simply Byzantium. Its capital was Constantinople (now Istanbul).

Caliph – in Arabic *Khalifah*, a successor of Prophet Muhammad who took responsibility and ruled on behalf of Allah and his messenger.

The plural for *Khalifah* is *Khulafa*.

Caucasus – the land of Sultan Muhammad Uzbeg Khan of the Golden Horde, a mountainous area between the Black Sea and the Caspian Sea, includes parts of Russia, Georgia, Azerbaijan, Armenia, Turkey and Iran. It has the highest peaks in Europe.

Chishtiyah – an important and famous spiritual *tariqah* (path) named after a famous Sufi of India, the saint Shaykh Muin al-Din Chishti. See Sufi Orders.

Creed – a set of systematic beliefs that influences the way a person lives, or a statement of faith.

Crusades – the eight massive attempts of many armies under Christianity to reconquer Jerusalem from the Muslims.

Dar al-uloom – lit. a house of knowledge; an Islamic seminary for higher education in Islam.

Euclid – a Greek mathematician who lived in Alexandria, Egypt around 300BCE. Often referred to as the Father of Geometry. He wrote the influential 'Elements' - a comprehensive book of all the known mathematics of his time and the earliest known discussion of geometry.

Exegesis – commentary of the Qur'an. See *tafsir*.

Existentialism – the philosophical belief which states that humans are responsible for creating meaning and purpose in their lives. This the opposite of essentialism which states that the purpose of life has been fixed at birth.

Falasifah – philosophers, *falsafah* is Arabic for philosophy.

Fallible – to make mistakes, someone who can sin.

Fatimid – a dynasty of Muslim rulers in Egypt (10th - 12th century) who were descendants from Fatimah, the daughter of the Prophet.

Fatwa – a legal ruling, guidance from a Mufti (an expert religious scholar who issues a *fatwa* on any matter of Islamic law). The plural is fatawa. See *Mufti*.

Feudalism – a legal system in Europe for structuring society based on having land in exchange for labour.

Fiqh – lit. to understand; the study of Islamic law and jurisprudence.

A specialist in Islamic law is a *faqih*, a scholar, sometimes called *Imam*. The plural is *fuqaha*.

Franks – a Germanic people who originated along the lower Rhine River. A powerful Christian kingdom after the western Roman Empire. They dominated parts of France, Belgium and Germany. The name France (Francia) is derived from their name.

Galen – a medical doctor (129-200 CE), his philosophy (Galenic thought) influenced the medieval period, a great intellectual of Western antiquity who wrote extensively.

Gnosis – spiritual awareness, knowledge of Allah, experiential knowledge. See *ma'rifa*.

Hasan – lit. good; a category of *hadith*. See *sahih*, *mawdu*.

Heliocentric theory – a cosmological model where the sun is assumed to be near a central point while the earth rev Hellenistic thought – the different philosophical schools of the Hellenistic period (323 -30 BCE) in the Greek speaking world.

Hellenistic thought – the different philosophical schools of the Hellenistic period (323 -30 BCE) in the Greek speaking world.

Heresiology – this is the study of heresies. Heresies are beliefs that are against orthodox or traditionally accepted beliefs and doctrines.

Heretical – to belief or have a view which is against what is generally and normally accepted.

Herodotus – the ancient Greek historian (484 - 430/425 BCE).

Ijtihad – lit. to struggle, make the greatest effort; refers to the use of reason to find an appropriate ruling on a matter not directly ruled by the Qur'an. It is an intellectual effort.

Ikhtilaf – lit. difference; usually differences of opinion on religious matters and juristic issues.

Ikhwan al-Safa – The Brotherhood of Purity, a secret society in Basra. It was forum for discussions, published the Treaties of The Brotherhood of Purity (*Rasa'il Ikhwan as- Safa*).

Ilm al-kalam – the study of Divine Speech, or speculative Islamic theology. *Kalam Allah* means the word and speech of Allah. See *kalam*.

Indus – Indus Valley area around one of the longest rivers (Indus), location of the world's first large civilisations around the area of modern-day Pakistan and Northern India.

Ishraqi – from the Arabic *ishraq* meaning illumination; a follower or philosopher of the school of philosophy of Shaykh Shihab al-Din Suhrawardi. See Suhrawardiyya, Sufi Orders.

Islamic Fertile Crescent – or Cradle of Civilisation; the region in the Middle East from the Persian Gulf to southern Iraq, northern Egypt, Jordan, Palestine, Israel, Syria, parts of Iran and Türkiye.

Johannes Kepler (1571-1630 CE) – a German astronomer and mathematician most famous for his three laws of planetary motion (1) The planets move in elliptical orbits around the Sun (2) the speed of each planet varies (3) the Sun is responsible for that variation.

Jurisprudence – *fiqh*, law, Muslim legal system, there are four main schools (*madhhab*) of jurisprudence among the Sunni communities.

Jurist – an expert in law, a person trained in *fiqh* and *Sharia (no italics)*. See *faqih*.

Kalam – lit. speech; applied to Islamic theology which is the study of Divine Speech. These theologians were called *ahl al-kalam*, Imams or scholars of *kalam* or *mutakallimun*.

Karramiyah – believe Allah has a body, has limited power, their intellectual center was in Nishapur, taught that a verbal declaration of faith was enough to someone a believer, emphasised an ascetic and communal lifestyle, founded by Muhammad ibn Karram (d.896 CE/255AH).

Khilafah – the concept of taking responsibility or ruling in Allah's name and according to His rules. A religious and political leader of Islam. See Caliph.

Khwajah – an honorific title meaning master, mainly used for Sufi teachers.

Khanqah – see Zawiyah.

Maliki madhhab – the school of jurisprudence (*fiqh*) as explained by Malik ibn Anas of Madinah.

Mamluk – the descendants of Turkish and Circassian slave-soldiers who were military rulers in Egypt. Their dynasty lasted from 1252 to 1517 CE when it was defeated by the Ottomans.

Mantiq – lit. logic or speech; a science whose principles protect from making errors. It involves studying definitions and proofs. It enables accurate and clear thinking. It has three parts: conceptualisation, judgement and reasoning.

Manuscript – original copy of work before it is printed. It may be bound as a book, a scroll or consist of loose pages. Some are decorated with pictures, border decorations, embossed initial letters or full-page illustrations. Manuscript is abbreviated as MS.

Marinid monarch – a tribal group, Arabised Berber dynasty of 1244 CE mainly in Morocco. Sultan Abu Inan Faris was one their rulers, Fez was their capital, they defeated the last Almohads.

Mawlawiyyah Order – taken from *mawlana*, a title of Mawlana Rumi. See *Mevlavi*.

Mazdakism – a Magian priest in Persia who led a cult within Zoroastrian Mazdaeism. He preached that evil was equal to good. Light and darkness got mixed to create the world.

Medieval period – the period in Europe of expansion, centralisation and political disruption and violence, resulting in the foundation of many modern European countries. It was also dominated by a surge in Christianity by building cathedrals, clearing land by peasants, settling of new towns and villages, and building of great castles by local nobility. See Middle Ages.

Metaphysics – is a major work of Aristotle. In it he developed the doctrine of First Philosophy. It is one of the greatest philosophical works and its influence on the Greeks, the Muslims and other philosophers was huge.

Mevlavi – A Sufi order guided by Mawlana Jalal al-Din al-Rumi in Konya, Türkiye. See Sufi Orders.

Middle Ages – the period in European history between the fall of the Rome in 476 CE to the period of the Renaissance in the 13th, 14th, or 15th century.

Mongols – warriors from Central Asia who swept through Islamic lands in the 13th and 14th centuries causing massive destruction. The most famous were Genghis Khan, Hulago and Timur.

Mujtahid – one who was qualified to practice *ijtihad*, they have vast and deep knowledge and specialise in Islam. They make original judgements. See *ijtihad*.

Mutakallimun – *kalam* means speech. Theologians who study Divine Speech, justice, hell, and reject falsehood and defend Islam. See *kalam*, *Mu'tazila*, *Ashariyyah*.

Mutasawwifin – people who have taken the path of Sufism to get closer to Allah. See Sufism.

Mystic – a person who follows a spiritual path or Sufi Order for self-purification. See Sufism.

Mysticism – the inner dimension, a path for spiritual knowledge and purity. See Sufism.

Neoplatonic – this is a philosophical system which started after Plato and is grounded in the teachings of Plotinus. It argued that this world is only a copy of an ideal reality which lies beyond this material world.

Orthodoxy – the generally accepted beliefs which do not depart from the original tradition. See heterodoxy.

Pantheistic beliefs – the belief that the universe as a whole is God. It claims that God includes the universe as a part of it, though not the whole of His being.

Peripatetic – a philosophical school which follow broadly the Greek tradition. It involves thinking while walking. Plato would invite his student Aristotle for contemplative walks.

Persia – This is ancient Iran. The term Persia was used for centuries, mainly in the West, to designate those regions where Persian language and culture dominated. The region of modern Iran. The Persian language is also known by Farsi or Parsi.

Philosophy – it is a form of rational and intellectual inquiry, it aims to be systematic, it tends to critically reflect on its own methods. The study of knowledge, reason, language and existence.

Qadi – usually a judge appointed by a ruler or a government on the basis of the extensive knowledge of Islamic law. The decision of a *qadi* is final.

Qadiriyah – an important and famous spiritual *tariqah* (path) named after a famous Sufi of Baghdad, the saint Shaykh Abd al-Qadir al-Jilani. It is popular from India to Morocco. It is also known as Jilalah in the Arab West. See Sufi Orders.

Rationalism – a school of thought which applied reason to the solutions of philosophical problems. See Mu'tazila.

Sahih – lit. correct, sound; usually refers to a *Hadith* which is authentic. See Hasan.

Sanskrit – the ancient language in Hinduism. It was used as a means of communication by the Hindu Heavenly Gods. Sanskrit is also used in Jainism, Buddhism, and Sikhism. It is a complex language with vast vocabulary. It is used in reading sacred texts.

Seljuks – a dynasty of a Turkic people (1037-1194 CE), their ancestral leader was Seljuk (Saljuq), their Oghuz clans converted to Islam in the eleventh century.

Sufi lodge – usually a place of religious retreat. See Sufism, Zawiya.

Sufi Order – a path of guidance to spiritual purification and character development to get closer to Allah and develop His love. There are many methods (Sufi Orders). See Naqshbandiyyah, Chishtiyah, Murabitun, Qadiriyah, Suhrawardiyya, Tijaniyya and others. See Sufism.

Sufism – in Arabic *Tasawwuf*, probably derived from *safa* meaning purity or *suf* meaning wool (simple garments). Sufism is often called Islamic mysticism or spirituality. It emphasises purification of the *nafs*, heart, mind, actions by developing piety, devotion, religiousness, *zikr*, and constant awareness of Allah. See Sufi, Sufi Order.

Tafsir – to explain and give commentary on the meaning of the verses of the Qur'an.

Tasawwuf – Islamic spirituality. See Sufism, Sufi, Sufi Order.

Teleological – the use of arguments to explain the existence of Allah in terms of the purpose they serve rather than of the cause. It relates to the belief of design and purpose in the world.

Transoxiana – included as the oldest states in Central Asia. It was located around the river Amu Darya (the River Oxus). Its territory varied depending on its ruler. It stretched into Afghanistan, eastern

Iran, central Turkmenistan and parts of Kyrgyzstan, Uzbekistan and all of Tajikistan.

Ulum al-aqliyah – philosophical sciences like logic, mathematics, philosophy and medicine.

Zahiri – meaning literal and apparent; a school of law which adopts literally meanings as opposed to allegorical or mystical interpretation of texts. Now almost extinct.

Zangid dynasty – a Muslim Turkic dynasty founded by Zangi. It ruled northern Iraq and Syria in the period 1127-1222 CE. After Zangi's death, Syria went to Nur al-Din and Al-Jazirah to Sayf al-Din Ghazi. They led the first counterattacks against the Crusades.

Zawiyah – In North Africa, it means an oratory or small mosque, a meeting place for Sufis for prayer or *zikr*. It may be a small or large or even a mausoleum of a saint. It is equivalent to *khanqah* in the East or *tekke* or *dargah* in Turkey. Also, part of a room set aside for prayer. See Sufi lodge.

Zuhd – abstinence, austerity, asceticism, not setting one's heart on worldly things. It involves living simply, not clinging to personal possessions such as wealth, food, clothes, name or fame. It is being devoted and disciplined to strengthen spirituality and Godliness.